W9-CFQ-367

THE BEST OF
ROBERT SERVICE

ILLUSTRATED EDITION

Copyright 1983, 1990 by Running Press
All rights reserved under the Pan-American
and International Copyright Conventions.

Printed in China.

*This book may not be reproduced in whole or in part
in any form or by any means, electronic or mechanical,
including photocopying, recording, or by any information
storage and retrieval system now known or hereafter
invented, without written permission from the publisher.*

9 8 7
Digit on the right indicates the number of this printing.

Library of Congress Control Number 2002116207

ISBN 0-7624-1631-9

Jacket and interior designed by Serrin Bodmer
Photo research by Susan Oyama
Cover and interior photographs by Clarke & Clarence
Kinsey, Grand Forks, Yukon Territory, © Copyright 2003,
Ronald C. Kinsey, Jr., Seattle, Washington.

This book may be ordered by mail from the publisher.
Please add $2.50 for postage and handling for each copy.
But try your bookstore first!

Published by Courage Books,
an imprint of
Running Press Book Publishers
125 South Twenty-second Street
Philadelphia, Pennsylvania 19103-4399

Visit us on the web!
www.runningpress.com

TABLE OF CONTENTS

PREFACE

Robert W. Service was born on January 14, 1874, in Preston, a city about 25 miles north-northeast of Liverpool, and spent his boyhood in Glasgow. After graduating from school, he was apprenticed as a bank clerk. But like one of the young men in his "Rhyme of the Restless Ones," he soon grew impatient, sailed to Canada, and spent the next years working at odd jobs up and down the coast of the Pacific Northwest. Finally, in 1904, he accepted the conventional job of bank teller in the highly unconventional town of Whitehorse. Later, the Canadian Bank of Commerce transferred him to its branch in the formerly rip-roaring town of Dawson, where he inhabited a snug bungalow much like the one described in "The Little Old Log Cabin." By then, the frenetic days of the Gold Rush were over, but Service took the yarns and stories he had overheard and transformed them into the stuff of myth and legend.

In 1907, Service published his first collection of poetry, *Songs of a Sourdough*, in London. That same year, Philadelphia's Edward Stern and Company published it in the United States under the title of *The Spell of the Yukon and Other Verses*. This eclectic little volume included narratives of the New York waterfront and European painters, together with "The Shooting of Dan McGrew" and "The Cremation of Sam McGee," which were to become two of the most-memorized poems in the language.

In its various editions, the book was a huge success, earning enough royalties to let Service quit his bank job once and for all in 1909—the same year Stern and Company published his second, longer collection, *Ballads of a Cheechako*,

which further enlarged his vivid roster of north-land scamps and scoundrels.

But only in these two books did Service depict the Yukon's heady, lawless Gold Rush days. During World War I, Service's chronic wanderlust led him to the Balkans as a correspondent for the *Toronto Star*, to the South Seas, and eventually to France, where he made his home until his death in 1958. All told, he published more than two dozen volumes of fiction, poetry, and autobiography. But his fame rests squarely on the vibrant, energetic, and matchlessly colorful poems in *The Spell of the Yukon* and *Ballads of a Cheechako*.

Here, we have re-arranged the poems of the original Stern and Company editions so that, for the first time, they create a chronological saga of the Gold Rush. After acquainting yourself with "The Men Who Don't Fit In," you can travel the harrowing "Trail of Ninety-Eight" to "The Land God Forgot," sharing the heartbreaks and exultations of prospecting as well as the tall tales and con games of the likes of Gum-Boot Ben. Here, too, are hints of the supernatural (in the ballads of "One-Eyed Mike," and "The Black Fox Skin") and the aching loneliness that made sourdoughs like Hard-Luck Henry dream of a wife and children. Yet once bedded down in civilized comfort, the ex-Yukoner soon longs for the wild again ("The Lure of Little

Voices")—and returns to face "The Law of the Yukon" and his own final showdown with the physical and mental hazards of the frozen north.

Service was clearly influenced by "The Rime of the Ancient Mariner," and, like Coleridge, favored internal rhymes—often tucked into extremely long verses. From the start, publishers have printed these extra-long lines as they would ordinary prose, letting them break whenever they reached the right-hand margin of the page. In this book, we have broken each of Service's lengthy verses according to its meter—which makes the poems much easier to read, either silently or aloud.

Even so, readers may wonder what a cheechako is and puzzle over Scots-dialect words like shoon, archaic "poetic" terms like empery, and Yukonisms like muckluck and Siwach—without realizing that Service employs them with ingenious care. For example, when Dangerous Dan McGrew decides to "make it a spread misère," he is intentionally setting himself up to lose at cards—a detail that adds an ironic foreshadowing to his impending fate. But no longer will readers lack this kind of information: at the back of this book, you'll find a complete glossary of Service's more exotic words and phrases.

Here, then, is Robert W. Service's most memorable, quotable work—newly arranged and ready to enchant a whole new generation of readers.

—Tam Mossman, Editor
Philadelphia, 1983

L'Envoi
[1907]

You who have lived in the land,
   You who have trusted the trail,
You who are strong to withstand,
   You who are swift to assail:
      Songs have I sung to beguile,
       Vintage of desperate years,
      Hard as a harlot's smile,
      Bitter as unshed tears.

Little of joy nor mirth,
   Little of ease I sing;
Sagas of men of earth
   Humanly suffering,
      Such as you all have done;
      Savagely faring forth,
      Sons of the midnight sun,
      Argonauts of the North.

Far in the land God forgot
   Glimmers the lure of your trail;
Still in your lust are you taught
   Even to win is to fail.
      Still must you follow and fight
      Under the vampire wing;
      There in the long, long night
      Hoping and vanquishing.

Husbandmen of the Wild,
   Reaping a barren gain;
Scourged by desire, reconciled
   Unto disaster and pain;
      These, my songs, are for you,
      You who are seared with the brand
      God knows I have tried to be true;
      Please God you will understand.

To the Man of the High North

My rhymes are rough, and often in my rhyming
  I've drifted, silver-sailed, on seas of dream,
Hearing afar the bells of Elfland chiming,
  Seeing the groves of Arcadie agleam.
I was the thrall of Beauty that rejoices
  From peak snow-diademed to regal star;
Yet to mine aerie ever pierced the voices,
  The pregnant voices of the Things That Are.

The Here, the Now, the vast Forlorn around us;
  The gold-delirium, the ferine strife;
The lusts that lure us on, the hates that hound us;
  Our red rags in the patchwork quilt of Life.

The nameless men who nameless rivers travel,
  And in strange valleys greet strange deaths alone;
The grim, intrepid ones who would unravel
  The mysteries that shroud the Polar Zone.

These will I sing, and if one of you linger
  Over my pages in the Long, Long Night,
And on some lone line lay a calloused finger,
  Saying: "It's human—true—it hits me right;"
Then will I count this loving toil well spent;
Then will I dream awhile—content, content.

The Men That Don't Fit In

There's a race of men that don't fit in,
    A race that can't stay still;
So they break the hearts of kith and kin,
    And they roam the world at will
They range the field and they rove the flood,
    And they climb the mountain's crest.
Theirs is the curse of the gypsy blood,
    And they don't know how to rest.

If they just went straight, they might go far;
    They are strong and brave and true;
But they're always tired of the things that are,
    And they want the strange and new.
They say: "Could I find my proper groove,
    What a deep mark I would make!"
So they chop and change, and each fresh move
    Is only a fresh mistake.

And each forgets, as he strips and runs
    With a brilliant, fitful pace,
It's the steady, quiet, plodding ones
    Who win in the lifelong race.
And each forgets that his youth has fled,
    Forgets that his prime is past,
Till he stands one day, with a hope that's dead,
    In the glare of the truth at last.

He has failed, he has failed;
        he has missed his chance;
    He has just done things by half.
Life's been a jolly good joke on him,
    And now is the time to laugh.
Ha, ha! He is one of the Legion Lost;
    He was never meant to win.
He's a rolling stone, and it's bred in the bone;
    He's a man who won't fit in.

Spring cleanup provided a chance to see if the winter frost and ice had hidden any gold.

The Rhyme of the Restless Ones

We couldn't sit and study for the law;
   The stagnation of a bank we couldn't stand;
For our riot blood was surging,
     and we didn't need much urging
   To excitements and excesses that are banned.
So we took to wine and drink and other things,
   And the devil in us struggled to be free;
Till our friends rose up in wrath,
     and they pointed out the path,
And they paid our debts and packed us o'er the sea.

Oh, they shook us off and shipped us o'er the foam,
To the larger lands that lure a man to roam;
     And we took the chance they gave
     Of a far and foreign grave,
And we bade good-bye forevermore to home.

And some of us are climbing on the peak,
   And some of us are camping on the plain;
By pine and palm you'll find us,
     with never claim to bind us,
   By track and trail you'll meet us once again.

We are fated serfs to freedom—sky and sea;
   We have failed where slummy cities overflow;
But the stranger ways of earth
     know our pride and know our worth,
And we go into the dark as fighters go.

Yes, we go into the night as brave men go,
Though our faces they be often streaked with woe;
     Yet we're hard as cats to kill,
     And our hearts are reckless—still,
And we've danced with death a dozen times or so.

And you'll find us in Alaska after gold,
   And you'll find us herding cattle in the South.
We like strong drink and fun,
     and, when the race is run,
   We often die with curses in our mouth.
We are wild as colts unbroke, but never mean.
   Of our sins we've shoulders broad to bear the blame
But we'll never stay in town
     and we'll never settle down,
   And we'll never have an object or an aim.

No, there's that in us that time can never tame;
And life will always seem a careless game;
     And they'd better far forget—
     Those who say they love us yet—
Forget, blot out with bitterness our name.

The Younger Son

If you leave the gloom of London
    and you seek a glowing land,
  Where all except the flag is strange and new,
There's a bronzed and stalwart fellow
    who will grip you by the hand,
  And greet you with a welcome warm and true;
For he's your younger brother, the one you sent away
  Because there wasn't room for him at home;
And now he's quite contented, and
    he's glad he didn't stay,
  And he's building Britain's greatness o'er the foam.

When the giant herd is moving
    at the rising of the sun,
  And the prairie is lit with rose and gold,
And the camp is all abustle, and the busy day's begun,
  He leaps into the saddle sure and bold.
Through the round of heat and hurry,
    through the racket and the rout,
  He rattles at a pace that nothing mars;
And when the night-winds whisper
    and camp-fires flicker out,
  He is sleeping like a child beneath the stars.

When the wattle-blooms are drooping
    in the somber shed-oak glade,
  And the breathless land is lying in a swoon,
He leaves his work a moment,
    leaning lightly on his spade,
  And he hears the bell-bird chime the Austral noon.
The parrakeets are silent in the gum-tree by the creek;
  The ferny grove is sunshine-steeped and still;
But the dew will gem the myrtle
    in the twilight ere he seek
  His little lonely cabin on the hill.

Around the purple, vine-clad slope
    the argent river dreams;
  The roses almost hide the house from view.
A snow-peak of the Winterberg
    in crimson splendor gleams;
  The shadow deepens down on the karroo.
He seeks the lily-scented dusk
    beneath the orange tree;
  His pipe in silence glows and fades and glows;
And then two little maids come out
    and climb upon his knee,
  And one is like the lily, one the rose.

He sees his white sheep dapple
    o'er the green New Zealand plain,
  And where Vancouver's shaggy ramparts frown,
When the sunlight threads the pine-gloom
    he is fighting might and main
  To clinch the rivets of an Empire down.
You will find him toiling, toiling,
    in the south or in the west,
  A child of nature, fearless, frank and free;
And the warmest heart that beats for you
    is beating in his breast,
  And he sends you loyal greeting o'er the sea.

You've a brother in the army,
    you've another in the Church;
  One of you is a diplomatic swell;
You've had the pick of everything
    and left him in the lurch,
  And yet I think he's doing very well.
I'm sure his life is happy,
    and he doesn't envy yours;
  I know he loves the land his pluck has won;
And I fancy in the years unborn,
    while England's fame endures,
She will come to bless with pride—the Younger Son.

Occasionally miners would stop for a while at a claim and then move on.
Sometimes they stayed with family and friends who were already in the North,
or found lodging with fellow miners they befriended while working the claims.

The Three Voices

The waves have a story to tell me,
    As I lie on the lonely beach;
Chanting aloft in the pine-tops,
    The wind has a lesson to teach;
But the stars sing an anthem of glory
    I cannot put into speech.

The waves tell of ocean spaces,
    Of hearts that are wild and brave,
Of populous city places,
    Of desolate shores they lave,
Of men who sally in quest of gold
    To sink in an ocean grave.

The wind is a mighty roamer;
    He bids me keep me free,
Clean from the taint of the gold-lust,
    Hardy and pure as he;
Cling with my love to nature,
    As a child to the mother-knee.

But the stars throng out in their glory,
    And they sing of the God in man;
They sing of the Mighty Master,
    Of the loom his fingers span,
Where a star or a soul is a part of the whole
    And weft in the wondrous plan.

Here by the camp-fire's flicker,
    Deep in my blanket curled,
I long for the peace of the pine-gloom,
    When the scroll of the Lord is unfurled
And the wind and the wave are silent,
    And world is singing to world.

The Call of the Wild

Have you gazed on naked grandeur
      where there's nothing else to gaze on,
  Set pieces and drop-curtain scenes galore,
Big mountains heaved to heaven,
      which the blinding sunsets blazon,
  Black canyons where the rapids rip and roar?
Have you swept the visioned valley
      with the green stream streaking through it,
  Searched the Vastness for a something you have lost?
Have you strung your soul to silence?
      Then for God's sake go and do it;
  Hear the challenge, learn the lesson, pay the cost.

Have you wandered in the wilderness,
      the sagebrush desolation,
  The bunch-grass levels where the cattle graze?
Have you whistled bits of ragtime
      at the end of all creation,
  And learned to know the desert's little ways?
Have you camped upon the foothills,
      have you galloped o'er the ranges,
  Have you roamed the arid sun-lands through and through?
Have you chummed up with the mesa?
      Do you know its moods and changes?
  Then listen to the Wild—it's calling you.

Have you known the Great White Silence,
      not a snow-gemmed twig aquiver?
  (Eternal truths that shame our soothing lies.)
Have you broken trail on snowshoes,
      mushed your huskies up the river,
  Dared the unknown, led the way, and clutched the prize?

Have you marked the map's void spaces,
      mingled with the mongrel races,
  Felt the savage strength of brute in every thew?
And though grim as hell the worst is,
      can you round it off with curses?
  Then hearken to the Wild—it's wanting you.
Have you suffered, starved, and triumphed,
      groveled down, yet grasped at glory,
  Grown bigger in the bigness of the whole?
"Done things" just for the doing,
      letting babblers tell the story,
  Seeing through the nice veneer the naked soul?
Have you seen God in His splendors,
      heard the text that nature renders
  (You'll never hear it in the family pew.)
The simple things, the true things,
      the silent men who do things?
  Then listen to the Wild—it's calling you.

They have cradled you in custom,
      they have primed you with their preaching,
  They have soaked you in convention through and through;
They have put you in a showcase;
      you're a credit to their teaching.
  But can't you hear the Wild?—it's calling you.

Let us probe the silent places,
      let us seek what luck betides us;
  Let us journey to a lonely land I know.
There's a whisper on the night-wind,
      there's a star agleam to guide us,
  And the Wild is calling, calling . . . let us go.

The Song of the Mouth-Organ

(With apologies to the singer of the "Song of the Banjo.")

I'm a homely little bit of tin and bone;
    I'm beloved by the Legion of the Lost.
I haven't got a "vox humana" tone,
    And a dime or two will satisfy my cost.
I don't attempt your high-falutin' flights;
    I am more or less uncertain on the key;
But I tell you, boys, there's lots and lots of nights
    When you've taken mighty comfort out of me.

I weigh an ounce or two, and I'm so small
    You can pack me in the pocket of your vest;
And when at night so wearily you crawl
    Into your bunk and stretch your limbs to rest,
You take me out and play me soft and low,
    The simple songs that trouble your heartstrings;
The tunes you used to fancy long ago,
    Before you made a rotten mess of things.

Then a dreamy look will come into your eyes,
    And you break off in the middle of a note;
And then, with just the dreariest of sighs,
    You drop me in the pocket of your coat.
But somehow I have bucked you up a bit;
    And, as you turn around and face the wall,
You don't feel quite so spineless and unfit—
    You're not so bad a fellow after all.

Do you recollect the bitter Arctic night;
   Your camp beside the canyon on the trail;
Your tent a tiny square of orange light;
   The moon above consumptive-like and pale;
Your supper cooked, your little stove aglow;
   You tired, but snug and happy as a child?
Then 'twas "Turkey in the Straw"
      till your lips were nearly raw,
   And you hurled your bold defiance at the Wild.

Do you recollect the flashing, lashing pain;
   The gulf of humid blackness overhead;
The lightning making rapiers of the rain,
   The cattle-horns like candles of the dead;
You sitting on your bronco there alone,
   In your slicker, saddle-sore and sick with cold?
Do you think the silent herd
      did not hear "The Mocking Bird,"
   Or relish "Silver Threads among the Gold"?

Do you recollect the wild Magellan coast;
   The headwinds and the icy, roaring seas;
The nights you thought that everything was lost,
   The days you toiled in water to your knees;
The frozen ratlines shrieking in the gate;
   The hissing steeps and gulfs of livid foam:
When you cheered your messmates nine
      with "Ben Bolt" and "Clementine,"
   And "Dixie Land" and "Seeing Nellie Home"?

Let the jammy banjo voice the Younger Son,
   Who waits for his remittance to arrive.
I represent the grimy, gritty one,
   Who sweats his bones to keep himself alive;
Who's up against the real thing from his birth;
   Whose heritage is hard and bitter toil.
I voice the weary, smeary ones of earth,
   The helots of the sea and of the soil.

I'm the Steinway of strange mischief and mischance;
   I'm the Stradivarius of blank defeat;
In the down-world, when the devil leads the dance,
   I am simply and symbolically meet.
I'm the irrepressive spirit of mankind;
   I'm the small boy playing knuckle down with Death;
At the end of all things known,
      where God's rubbish-heap is thrown,
   I shrill impudent triumph at a breath.

I'm a humble little bit of tin and horn;
   I'm a byword, I'm a plaything, I'm a jest.
The virtuoso looks on me with scorn,
   But there's times when I am better than the best.
Ask the stoker and the sailor of the sea;
   Ask the mucker and the hewer of the pine;
Ask the herder of the plain,
      ask the gleaner of the grain—
   There's a lowly, loving kingdom—and it's mine.

These happy faces belong to some of the richest miners in the Klondike—the Berry brothers from California, who were said to have taken a million dollars or more from their Eldorado claims.

The Trail of 'Ninety-Eight

Gold! We leapt from our benches.
    Gold! We sprang from our stools.
Gold! We wheeled in the furrow,
    fired with the faith of fools.
Fearless, unfound, unfitted,
    far from the night and the cold,
Heard we the clarion summons,
    followed the master-lure—Gold!

Men from the sands of the Sunland;
    men from the woods of the West;
Men from the farms and the cities,
    into the Northland we pressed.
Graybeards and striplings and women,
    good men and bad men and bold,
Leaving our homes and our loved ones,
    crying exultantly, "Gold!"

Never was seen such an army,
    pitiful, futile, unfit;
Never was seen such a spirit,
    manifold courage and grit.
Never has been such a cohort
    under one banner unrolled
As surged to the ragged-edged Arctic,
    urged by the arch-tempter—Gold.

"Farewell!" we cried to our dearests;
    little we cared for their tears.
"Farewell!" we cried to the humdrum
    and the yoke of the hireling years;
Just like a pack of school-boys,
    and the big crowd cheered us good-bye.
Never were hearts so uplifted,
    never were hopes so high.
The spectral shores flitted past us,

and every whirl of the screw
    Hurled us nearer to fortune,
        and ever we planned what we'd do—
Do with the gold when we got it—
        big, shiny nuggets like plums,
There in the sand of the river,
        gouging it out with our thumbs.

And one man wanted a castle,
        another a racing stud;
    A third would cruise in a palace yacht
        like a red-necked prince of blood.
And so we dreamed and we vaunted,
        millionaires to a man,
Leaping to wealth in our visions
        long ere the trail began.

II.

We landed in wind-swept Skagway.
        We joined the weltering mass,
Clamoring over their outfits,
        waiting to climb the Pass.
We tightened our girths and our pack-straps;
        we linked on the Human Chain,
Struggling up to the summit,
        where every step was a pain.

Gone was the joy of our faces,
        grim and haggard and pale;
The heedless mirth of the shipboard
        was changed to the care of the trail.
We flung ourselves in the struggle,
        packing our grub in relays,
Step by step to the summit

in the bale of the winter days.
Floundering deep in the sump-holes,
        stumbling out again;
    Crying with cold and weakness,
        crazy with fear and pain.
Then from the depths of our travail,
        ere our spirits were broke,
    Grim, tenacious and savage,
        the lust of the trail awoke.

For grub meant gold to our thinking,
        and all that could walk must pack;
    The sheep for the shambles stumbled,
        each with a load on its back;
And even the swine were burdened,
        and grunted and squealed and rolled,
And men went mad in the moment,
        huskily clamoring, "Gold!"

"Klondike or bust!" rang the slogan;
        every man for his own.
Oh, how we flogged the horses,
        staggering skin and bone!
Oh, how we cursed their weakness,
        anguish they could not tell,
    Breaking their hearts in our passion,
        lashing them on till they fell!

Oh, we were brutes and devils,
        goaded by lust and fear!
    Our eyes were strained to the summit;
        the weaklings dropped to the rear,
Falling in heaps by the trail-side,
        heart-broken, limp, and wan;
But the gaps closed up in an instant,

and heedless the chain went on.

Never will I forget it,
    there on the mountain face,
Antlike, men with their burdens,
    clinging in icy space;
Dogged, determined and dauntless,
    cruel and callous and cold,
Cursing, blaspheming, reviling,
    and ever that battle-cry—"Gold!"

Thus toiled we, the army of fortune,
    in hunger and hope and despair,
Till glacier, mountain and forest
    vanished, and, radiantly fair,
There at our feet lay Lake Bennett,
    and down to its welcome we ran:
The trail of the land was over,
    the trail of the water began.

III.

We built our boats and we launched them.
    Never has been such a fleet;
A packing-case for a bottom,
    a mackinaw for a sheet.
Shapeless, grotesque, lopsided,
    flimsy, makeshift and crude,
Each man after his fashion
    builded as best he could.

Each man worked like a demon,
    as prow to rudder we raced;
The winds of the Wild cried "Hurry!"
    the voice of the waters, "Haste!"

We hated those driving before us;
    we dreaded those pressing behind;
We cursed the slow current that bore us;
    we prayed to the God of the wind.

Spring! and the hillsides flourished,
    vivid in jewelled green;
Spring! and our hearts' blood nourished
    envy and hatred and spleen.
Little cared we for the Spring-birth;
    much cared we to get on—
Stake in the Great White Channel,
    stake ere the best be gone.

The greed of the gold possessed us;
    pity and love were forgot;
Covetous visions obsessed us;
    brother with brother fought.
Partner with partner wrangled,
    each one claiming his due;
Wrangled and halved their outfits,
    sawing their boats in two.

Thuswise we voyaged Lake Bennett,
    Tagish, then Windy Arm,
Sinister, savage and baleful,
    boding us hate and harm.
Many a scow was shattered
    there on that iron shore;
Many a heart was broken
    straining at sweep and oar.

We roused Lake Marsh with a chorus,
    we drifted many a mile.
There was the canyon before us—

cave-like its dark defile;
The shores swept faster and faster;
    the river narrowed to wrath;
Waters that hissed disaster
    reared upright in our path.

Beneath us the green tumult churning,
    above us the cavernous gloom;
Around us, swift twisting and turning,
    the black, sullen walls of a tomb.
We spun like a chip in a mill-race;
    our hearts hammered under the test;
Then—oh, the relief on each chill face!—
    we soared into sunlight and rest.

Hand sought for hand on the instant.
    Cried we, "Our troubles are o'er!"
Then, like a rumble of thunder,
    heard we a canorous roar.
Leaping and boiling and seething,
    saw we a cauldron afume;
There was the rage of the rapids,
    there was the menace of doom.

The river springs like a racer,
    sweeps through a gash in the rock;
Butts at the boulder-ribbed bottom,
    staggers and rears at the shock;
Leaps like a terrified monster,
    writhes in its fury and pain;
Then with the crash of a demon
    springs to the onset again.

Dared we that ravening terror;

heard we its din in our ears;
Called on the Gods of our fathers,
    juggled forlorn with our fears;
Sank to our waists in its fury,
    tossed to the sky like a fleece;
Then, when our dread was the greatest,
    crashed into safety and peace.

But what of the others that followed,
    losing their boats by the score?
Well could we see them and hear them,
    strung down that desolate shore.
What of the poor souls that perished?
    Little of them shall be said—
On to the Golden Valley!
    Pause not to bury the dead.

Then there were days of drifting,
    breezes soft as a sigh;
Night trailed her robe of jewels
    over the floor of the sky.
The moonlit stream was a python,
    silver, sinuous, vast,
That writhed on a shroud of velvet—
    well, it was done at last.

There were the tents of Dawson,
    there the scar of the slide;
Swiftly we poled o'er the shallows,
    swiftly leapt o'er the side.
Fires fringed the mouth of Bonanza;
    sunset gilded the dome;
The test of the trail was over—
    thank God, thank God, we were Home!

The Land
God Forgot

The lonely sunsets flare forlorn
    Down valleys dreadly desolate;
The lordly mountains soar in scorn
    As still as death, as stern as fate.

The lonely sunsets flame and die;
    The giant valleys gulp the night;
The monster mountains scrape the sky
    Where eager stars are diamond-bright.

So gaunt against the gibbous moon,
    Piercing the silence velvet-piled,
A lone wolf howls his ancient rune—
    The fell arch-spirit of the Wild.

O outcast land! O leper land!
    Let the lone wolf-cry all express
The hate insensate of thy hand,
    Thy heart's abysmal loneliness.

The Ballad of the
Northern Lights

One of the Down and Out—that's me.
    Stare at me well, aye, stare!
  Stare and shrink—say! you wouldn't think
    that I was a millionaire.
Look at my face, it's crimped and gouged—
    one of them death-mask things;
Don't seem the sort of man, do I,
    as might be the pal of kings?
Slouching along in smelly rags,
    a bleary-eyed, no-good bum;
A knight of the hollow needle, pard,
    spewed from the sodden slum.
Look me all over from head to foot;
    how much would you think I was worth?
A dollar? a dime? a nickel? Why,
    I'm the wealthiest man on earth!

No, don't you think that I'm off my base.
    You'll sing a different tune
If only you'll let me spin my yarn
    Come over to this saloon;
Wet my throat—it's as dry as chalk,
    and seeing as how it's you,
I'll tell the tale of a Northern trail,
    and so help me God, it's true.
I'll tell of the howling wilderness
    and the haggard Arctic heights,
Of a reckless vow that I made, and how
    I staked the Northern Lights.

Remember the year of the Big Stampede
    and the trail of 'Ninety-Eight?
When the eyes of the world were turned to the North
    and the hearts of men elate;

Hearts of the old dare-devil breed
    thrilled at the wondrous strike,
And to every man who could hold a pan
    came the message, "Up and hike"?
Well, I was there with the best of them,
    and I knew I would not fail.
You wouldn't believe it to see me now;
    but wait till you've heard my tale.

You've read of the trail of 'Ninety-Eight,
    but its woe no man may tell;
It was all of a piece and a whole yard wide,
    and the name of the brand was "Hell."
We heard the call and we staked our all;
    we were plungers playing blind,
And no man cared how his neighbor fared,
    and no man looked behind;
For a ruthless greed was born of need,
    and the weakling went to the wall,
And a curse might avail where a prayer would fail,
    and the gold-lust crazed us all.

Bold were we, and they called us three
    the "Unholy Trinity;"
There was Ole Olson, the sailor Swede,
    and the Dago Kid, and me.
We were the discards of the pack,
    the foreloopers of Unrest,
Reckless spirits of fierce revolt
    in the ferment of the West.
We were bound to win and we revelled in
    the hardships of the way.
We staked our ground and our hopes were crowned,
    and we hoisted out the pay.

We were rich in a day beyond our dreams,
 it was gold from the grass-roots down;
But we weren't used to such sudden wealth,
 and there was the Siren Town.
We were Crude and careless frontiersmen,
 with much in us of the beast;
We could bear the famine worthily,
 but we lost our heads at the feast.

The town looked mighty bright to us,
 with a bunch of dust to spend,
And nothing was half too good them days,
 and everyone was our friend.
Wining meant more than mining then,
 and life was a dizzy whirl,
Gambling and dropping chunks of gold
 down the neck of a dance-hall girl;
Till we went clean mad, it seems to me,
 and we squandered our last poke,
And we sold our claim, and we found ourselves
 one bitter morning—broke.

The Dago Kid he dreamed a dream
 of his mother's aunt who died—
In the dawn-light dim she came to him,
 and she stood by his bedside,
And she said: "Go forth to the highest North
 till a lonely trail ye find.
Follow it far and trust your star,
 and fortune will be kind."
But I jeered at him, and then there came
 the Sailor Swede to me,
And he said: "I dreamed of my sister's son,
 who croaked at the age of three.
From the herded dead he sneaked and said:
 'Seek you an Arctic trail.
'Tis pale and grim by the Polar rim,
 but seek and ye shall not fail.'"

And lo! that night I too did dream
 of my mother's sister's son,
And he said to me: "By the Arctic Sea
 there's a treasure to be won.
Follow and follow a lone moose trail,
 till you come to a valley grim,
On the slope of the lonely watershed
 that borders the Polar brim."
Then I woke my pals, and soft we swore
 by the mystic Silver Flail,
'Twas the hand of Fate, and to-morrow straight
 we would seek the lone moose trail.

We watched the groaning ice wrench free,
 crash on with a hollow din;
Men of the wilderness were we,
 freed from the taint of sin.
The mighty river snatched us up
 and it bore us swift along;
The days were bright, and the morning light
 was sweet with jewelled song.
We poled and lined up nameless streams,
 portaged o'er hill and plain;
We burnt our boat to save the nails,
 and built our boat again.

We guessed and groped, North, ever North,
 with many a twist and turn;
We saw ablaze in the deathless days
 the splendid sunsets burn.
O'er soundless lakes where the grayling makes
 a rush at the clumsy fly;
By bluffs so steep that the hard-hit sheep
 falls sheer from out the sky;
By lilied pools where the bull moose cools
 and wallows in huge content;
By rocky lairs where the pig-eyed bears
 peered at our tiny tent.
Through the black canyon's angry foam
 we hurled to dreamy bars,

And round in a ring the dog-nosed peaks
  bayed to the mocking stars.

Spring and summer and autumn went;
  the sky had a tallow gleam,
 Yet North and ever North we pressed
  to the land of our Golden Dream.
So we came at last to a tundra vast
  and dark and grim and lone;
 And there was the little lone moose trail,
  and we knew it for our own.
By muskeg hollow and nigger-head
  it wandered endlessly.
 Sorry of heart and sure of foot,
  weary men were we.
The short-lived sun had a leaden glare
  and the darkness came too soon,
 And stationed there with a solemn stare
  was the pinched, anemic moon.
Silence and silvern solitude
  till it made you dumbly shrink,
 And you thought to hear with an outward ear
  the things you thought to think.

Oh, it was wild and weird and wan,
  and ever in camp o' nights
 We would watch and watch the silver dance
  of the mystic Northern Lights.
And soft they danced from the Polar sky
  and swept in primrose haze;
 And swift they pranced with their silver feet,
  and pierced with a blinding blaze.
They danced a cotillion in the sky;
  they were rose and silver shod;
 It was not good for the eyes of man,
  'twas a sight for the eyes of God.
It made us mad and strange and sad,
  and the gold whereof we dreamed
 Was all forgot, and our only thought
  was of the lights that gleamed.

Oh, the tundra sponge it was golden brown,
  and some was a bright blood-red;
 And the reindeer moss gleamed here and there
  like the tombstones of the dead.
And in and out and around about
  the little trail ran clear,
 And we hated it with a deadly hate
  and we feared with a deadly fear.
And the skies of night were alive with light,
  with a throbbing, thrilling flame;
 Amber and rose and violet,
  opal and gold it came.
It swept the sky like a giant scythe,
  it quivered back to a wedge;
 Argently bright, it cleft the night
  with a wavy golden edge.
Pennants of silver waved and streamed,
  lazy banners unfurled;
 Sudden splendors of sabres gleamed,
  lightning javelins were hurled.
There in our awe we crouched and saw
  with our wild, uplifted eyes
 Charge and retire the hosts of fire
  in the battlefield of the skies.

But all things come to an end at last,
  and the muskeg melted away,
 And frowning down to bar our path
  a muddle of mountains lay.
And a gorge sheered up in granite walls,
  and the moose trail crept betwixt;
 'Twas as if the earth had gaped too far
  and her stony jaws were fixt.
Then the winter fell with a sudden swoop,
  and the heavy clouds sagged low,
 And earth and sky were blotted out
  in a whirl of driving snow.

We were climbing up a glacier
  in the neck of a mountain pass,

When the Dago Kid slipped down and fell
    into a deep crevasse.
When we got him out, one leg hung limp,
    and his brow was wreathed with pain,
And he says: "'Tis badly broken, boys,
    and I'll never walk again.
It's death for all if ye linger here,
    and that's no cursed lie;
Go on, go on while the trail is good,
    and leave me down to die."
He raved and swore, but we tended him
    with our uncouth, clumsy care.
The camp-fire gleamed and he gazed and dreamed
    with a fixed and curious stare.
Then all at once he grabbed my gun
    and he put it to his head,
And he says: "I'll fix it for you, boys"—
    them are the words he said.

So we sewed him up in a canvas sack
    and we slung him to a tree;
And the stars like needles stabbed our eyes,
    and woeful men were we.
And on we went on our woeful way,
    wrapped in a daze of dream
And the Northern Lights in the crystal nights
    came forth with a mystic gleam.
They danced and they danced the devil-dance
    over the naked snow;
And soft they rolled like a tide upshoaled
    with a ceaseless ebb and flow.
They rippled green with a wondrous sheen,
    they fluttered out like a fan;
They spread with a blaze of rose-pink rays
    never yet seen of man.
They writhed like a brood of angry snakes,
    hissing and sulphur pale;
Then swift they changed to a dragon vast,
    lashing a cloven tail.
It seemed to us, as we gazed aloft

with an everlasting stare,
The sky was a pit of bale and dread,
    and a monster revelled there.

We climbed the rise of a hog-back range
    that was desolate and drear,
When the Sailor Swede had a crazy fit,
    and he got to talking queer.
He talked of his home in Oregon
    and the peach trees all in bloom,
And the fern head-high, and the topaz sky,
    and the forests scented gloom.
He talked of the sins of his misspent life,
    and then he seemed to brood,
And I watched him there like a fox a hare,
    for I knew it was not good.
And sure enough, in the dim dawn-light
    I missed him from the tent,
And a fresh trail broke through the crusted snow,
    and I knew not where it went.
But I followed it o'er the seamless waste,
    and I found him at shut of day,
Naked there as a new-born babe—
    so I left him where he lay.

Day after day was sinister,
    and I fought fierce-eyed despair,
And I clung to life and I struggled on,
    I knew not why nor where.
I packed my grub in short relays,
    and I cowered down in my tent,
And the world around was purged of sound
    like a frozen continent.
Day after day was dark as death,
    but ever and ever at nights,
With a brilliancy that grew and grew,
    blazed up the Northern Lights.

They rolled around with a soundless sound
    like softly bruised silk;

They poured into the bowl of the sky
    with the gentle flow of milk.
In eager, pulsing violet
    their wheeling chariots came,
    Or they poised above the Polar rim
    like a coronal of flame.
From depths of darkness fathomless
    their lancing rays were hurled,
    Like the all-combining search-lights
    of the navies of the world.

There on the roof-pole of the world
    as one bewitched I gazed,
    And howled and grovelled like a beast
    as the awful splendors blazed.
My eyes were seared, yet thralled I peered
    through the parka hood, nigh blind;
    But I staggered on to the lights that shone,
    and never I looked behind.

There is a mountain round and low
    that lies by the Polar rim,
    And I climbed its height in a whirl of light,
    and I peered o'er its jagged brim;
And there in a crater deep and vast,
    ungained, unguessed of men,
    The mystery of the Arctic world
    was flashed into my ken.
For there these poor dim eyes of mine
    beheld the sight of sights—
    That hollow ring was the source and spring
    of the mystic Northern Lights.

Then I staked that place from crown to base,
    and I hit the homeward trail.
    Ah, God! it was good, though my eyes were blurred,
    and I crawled like a sickly snail.
In that vast white world where the silent sky
    communes with the silent snow,

In hunger and cold and misery
    I wandered to and fro.
But the Lord took pity on my pain,
    and He led me to the sea,
    And some ice-bound whalers heard my moan,
    and they fed and sheltered me.
They fed the feeble scarecrow thing
    that stumbled out of the wild
    With the ravaged face of a mask of death
    and the wandering wits of a child—
A craven, cowering bag of bones
    that once had been a man.
    They tended me and they brought me back
    to the world, and here I am.

Some say that the Northern Lights are the glare
    of the Arctic ice and snow;
    And some that it's electricity,
    and nobody seems to know.
But I'll tell you now—and if I lie,
    may my lips be stricken dumb—
    It's a *mine*, a mine of the precious stuff
    that men call radium.
It's a million dollars a pound, they say,
    and there's tons and tons in sight.
    You can see it gleam in a golden stream
    in the solitudes of night.
And it's mine, all *mine*—and say! if you
    have a hundred plunks to spare,
    I'll let you have the chance of your life,
    I'll sell you a quarter share.
You turn it down? Well, I'll make it ten,
    seeing as you are my friend.
    Nothing doing? Say! don't be hard—
    have you got a dollar to lend?
Just a dollar to help me out,
    I know you'll treat me white;
    I'll do as much for you some day . . .
    God bless you, sir; good-night!

Guests, employees, and owners take a break along the trail to pose in front of a symbol of Klondike elegance—a roadhouse with real glass windows and curtains.

Comfort

Say! You've struck a heap of trouble—
    Bust in business, lost your wife;
No one cares a cent about you,
    You don't care a cent for life;
Hard luck has of hope bereft you,
    Health is failing, wish you'd die—
Why, you've still the sunshine left you
    And the big, blue sky.

Sky so blue it makes you wonder
    If it's heaven shining through;
Earth so smiling 'way out yonder,
    Sun so bright it dazzles you;
Birds a-singing, flowers a-flinging
    All their fragrance on the breeze;
Dancing shadows, green, still meadows—
    Don't you mope, you've still got these.

These, and none can take them from you;
    These, and none can weigh their worth.
What! you're tired and broke and beaten?—
    Why, you're rich—you've got the earth!
Yes, if you're a tramp in tatters,
    While the blue sky bends above
You've got nearly all that matters—
    You've got God, and God is love.

The Ballad of Gum-Boot Ben

He was an old prospector with a vision bleared and dim.
He asked me for a grubstake, and the same I gave to him.
He hinted of a bidden trove, and when I made so bold
To question his veracity, this is the tale he told:

"I do not seek the copper streak,
    nor yet the yellow dust;
I am not fain for sake of gain
    to irk the frozen crust;
Let fellows gross find gilded dross,
    far other is my mark;
Oh, gentle youth, this is the truth—
    I go to seek the Ark.

"I prospected the Pelly bed,
    I prospected the White;
The Nordenscold for love of gold
    I piked from morn till night;
Afar and near for many a year
    I led the wild stampede,
Until I guessed that all my quest
    was vanity and greed.

"Then came I to a land I knew
    no man had ever seen,
A haggard land, forlornly spanned
    by mountains lank and lean;
The nitchies said 'twas full of dread,
    of smoke and fiery breath,
And no man dare put foot in there
    for fear of pain and death.

"But I was made all unafraid,
    so, careless and alone,
Day after day I made my way
    into that land unknown;
Night after night by camp-fire light
    I crouched in lonely thought;
Oh, gentle youth, this is the truth—
    I knew not what I sought.

"I rose at dawn; I wandered on.
    'Tis somewhat fine and grand
To be alone and hold your own
    in God's vast awesome land;
Come woe or weal, 'tis fine to feel
    a hundred miles between
The trails you dare and pathways where
    the feet of men have been.

"And so it fell on me a spell
    of wander-lust was cast.
The land was still and strange and chill,
    and cavernous and vast;
And sad and dead, and dull as lead,
    the valleys sought the snows;
And far and wide on every side
    the ashen peaks arose.

"The moon was like a silent spike
     that pierced the sky right through;
  The small stars popped and winked and hopped
     in vastitudes of blue;
And unto me for company
     came creatures of the shade,
  And formed in rings and whispered things
     that made me half afraid.

"And strange though be, 'twas borne on me
     that land had lived of old,
  And men had crept and slain and slept
     where now they toiled for gold;
Through jungles dim the mammoth grim
     had sought the oozy fen,
  And on his track, all bent of back,
     had crawled the hairy men.

"And furthermore, strange deeds of yore
     in this dead place were done.
  They haunted me, as wild and free
     I roamed from sun to sun;
Until I came where sudden flame
     uplit a terraced height,
A regnant peak that seemed to seek
     the coronal of night.

I scaled the peak; my heart was weak,
     yet on and on I pressed.
  Skyward I strained until I gained
     its dazzling silver crest;
And there I found, with all around
     a world supine and stark,
  Swept clean of snow, a flat plateau,
     and on it lay—the Ark.

"Yes, there, I knew, by two and two
     the beasts did disembark,
  And so in haste I ran and traced
     in letters on the Ark
My human name—Ben Smith's the same.
     And now I want to float
A syndicate to haul and freight
     to town that noble boat."

I met him later in a bar and made a gay remark
Anent on ancient miner and an option on the Ark.
He gazed at me reproachfully, as only topers can;
But what he said I can't repeat—he was a bad old man.

The Low-Down White

This is the pay-day up at the mines,
 when the bearded brutes come down
 There's money to burn in the streets to-night,
  so I've sent my klooch to town,
With a haggard face and a ribband of red
 entwined in her hair of brown.

And I know at the dawn she'll come reeling home
 with the bottles, one, two, three—
 One for herself, to drown her shame,
  and two big bottles for me,
To make me forget the thing I am
 and the man I used to be.

To make me forget the brand of the dog,
 as I crouch in this hideous place;
 To make me forget once I kindled the light
  of love in a lady's face,
Where even the squalid Siwash now
 holds me a black disgrace.

Oh, I have guarded my secret well!
 And who would dream as I speak
In a tribal tongue like a rogue unhung,

 'mid the ranchhouse filth and reek,
I could roll to bed with a Latin phrase
 and rise with a verse of Greek?

Yet I was a senior prizeman once,
 and the pride of a college eight;
 Called to the bar—my friends were true!
  but they could not keep me straight;
Then came the divorce, and I went abroad
 and "died" on the River Plate.

But I'm not dead yet; though with half a lung,
 there isn't time to spare,
 And I hope that the year will see me out,
  and, thank God, no one will care—
Save maybe the little slim Siwash girl
 with the rose of shame in her hair.

She will come with the dawn, and the dawn is near;
 I can see its evil glow,
 Like a corpse-light seen through a frosty pane
  in a night of want and woe;
And yonder she comes by the bleak bull-pines,
 swift staggering through the snow.

AFTER THE SPRING CLEAN UP.

KINSEY.

Spring cleanup was the best reason in the world to have a
party and no one could celebrate better than Klondikers.

The Man
from Eldorado

He's the man from Eldorado,
     and he's just arrived in town,
  In moccasins and oily buckskin shirt.
He's gaunt as any Indian, and pretty nigh as brown;
  He's greasy, and he smells of sweat and dirt.
He sports a crop of whiskers that would shame a healthy hog;
  Hard work has racked his joints and stooped his back;
He slops along the sidewalk followed by his yellow dog,
  But he's got a bunch of gold-dust in his sack.

He seems a little wistful as he blinks at all the lights,
  And maybe he is thinking of his claim
And the dark and dwarfish cabin
     where he lay and dreamed at nights,
  (Thank God, he'll never see the place again!)
Where he lived on tinned tomatoes,
     beef embalmed and sourdough bread,
  On rusty beans and bacon furred with mold;
His stomach's out of kilter and his system full of lead,
  But it's over, and his poke is full of gold.

He has panted at the windlass, he has loaded in the drift,
  He has pounded at the face of oozy clay;
He has taxed himself to sickness,
     dark and damp and double shift,
  He has labored like a demon night and day.
And now, praise God, it's over, and he seems to breathe again
  Of new-mown hay, the warm, wet, friendly loam;
He sees a snowy orchard in a green and dimpling plain,
  And a little vine-clad cottage, and it's—Home.

II.

He's the man from Eldorado,
   and he's had a bite and sup,
   And he's met in with a drouthy friend or two;
He's cached away his gold-dust, but he's sort of bucking up,
   So he's kept enough tonight to see him through.
His eye is bright and genial, his tongue no longer lags;
   His heart is brimming o'er with joy and mirth;
He may be far from savory, he may be clad in rags,
   But to-night he feels as if he owns the earth.

Says he, "Boys, here is where the shaggy
   North and I will shake;
   I thought I'd never manage to get free.
I kept on making misses; but at last I've got my stake;
   There's no more thawing frozen muck for me.
I am going to God's Country, where I'll live the simple life;
   I'll buy a bit of land and make a start;
I'll carve a little homestead, and I'll win a little wife,
   And raise ten little kids to cheer my heart."

They signified their sympathy by crowding to the bar;
   They bellied up three deep and drank his health.
He shed a radiant smile around and smoked a rank cigar;
   They wished him honor, happiness, and wealth.
They drank unto his wife to be—that unsuspecting maid;
   They drank unto his children half a score;
And when they got through drinking, very tenderly they laid
   The man from Eldorado on the floor.

III.

He's the man from Eldorado,
   and he's only starting in
   To cultivate a thousand-dollar jag.
His poke is full of gold-dust and his heart is full of sin,
   And he's dancing with a girl called Muckluck Mag.
She's as light as any fairy; she's as pretty as a peach;
   She's mistress of the witchcraft to beguile;
There's sunshine in her manner, there is music in her speech,
   And there's concentrated honey in her smile.

Oh, the fever of the dance-hall and the glitter and the shine,
   The beauty, and the jewels, and the whirl,
The madness of the music, the rapture of the wine,
   The languorous allurement of a girl!
She is like a lost madonna; he is gaunt, unkempt and grim;
   But she fondles him and gazes in his eyes;
Her kisses seek his heavy lips, and soon it seems to him
   He has staked a little claim in Paradise.

"Who's for a juicy two-step?" cries the master of the floor;
   The music throbs with soft, seductive beat.
There's glitter, gilt and gladness; there are pretty girls galore;
   There's a woolly man with moccasins on feet.
They know they've got him going; he is buying wine for all;
   They crowd around as buzzards at a feast,
Then when his poke is empty, they boost him from the hall,
   And spurn him in the gutter like a beast.

He's the man from Eldorado,
   and he's painting red the town;
   Behind he leaves a trail of yellow dust;
In a whirl of senseless riot he is ramping up and down;
   There's nothing checks his madness and his lust.
And soon the word is passed around—it travels like a flame;
   They fight to clutch his hand and call him friend,
The chevaliers of lost repute, the dames of sorry fame;
   Then comes the grim awakening—the end.

IV.

He's the man from Eldorado,
     and he gives a grand affair;
     There's feasting, dancing, wine without restraint.
The smooth Beau Brummels of the bar, the faro men, are there;
     The tinhorns and purveyors of red paint;
The sleek and painted women, their predacious eyes aglow
     Sure Klondike City never saw the like;
Then Muckluck Mag proposed the toast: "The giver of the show,
     The livest sport that ever hit the pike."

The "live one" rises to his feet; he stammers to reply—
     And then there comes before his muddled brain
A vision of green vastitudes beneath an April sky,
     And clover pastures drenched with silver rain.
He knows that it can never be, that he is down and out;
     Life leers at him with foul and fetid breath;
And then amid the revelry, the song and cheer and shout,
     He suddenly grows grim and cold as death.

He grips the table tensely, and he says, "Dear friends of mine,
     I've let you dip your fingers in my purse;
I've crammed you at my table,
     and I've drowned you in my wine,
And I've little left to give you but—my curse.
     I've failed supremely in my plans; it's rather late to whine;
My poke is mighty weasened up and small.
     I thank you each for coming here; the happiness is mine—
And now, you thieves and harlots, take it all."

V.

He twists the thong from off his poke; he swings it o'er his head;
     The nuggets fall around their feet like grain.
They rattle over roof and wall; they scatter, roll and spread;
     The dust is like a shower of golden rain.
The guests a moment stand aghast, then grovel on the floor;
     They fight, and snarl, and Claw, like beasts of prey;
And then, as everybody grabbed and everybody swore,
     The man from Eldorado slipped away.

He's the man from Eldorado,
     and they found him stiff and dead,
     Half covered by the freezing ooze and dirt.
A clotted Colt was in his hand, a hole was in his head,
     And he wore an old and oily buckskin shirt.
His eyes were fixed and horrible, as one who hails the end;
     The frost had set him rigid as a log;
And there, half lying on his breast, his last and only friend,
     There crouched and whined a mangy yellow dog.

The Reckoning

It's fine to have a blow-out in a fancy restaurant,
    With terrapin and canvas-back and all the wine you want;
To enjoy the flowers and music, watch the pretty women pass,
    Smoke a choice cigar, and sip the wealthy water in your glass.
It's bully in a high-toned joint to eat and drink your fill,
    But it's quite another matter when you
                              Pay the bill.
It's great to go out every night on fun or pleasure bent;
To wear your glad rags always and to never save a cent;
To drift along regardless, have a good time every trip;
To hit the high spots sometimes, and to let your chances slip;
To know you're acting foolish, yet to go on fooling still,
    Till Nature calls a show-down, and you
                              Pay the bill.
Time has got a little bill—get wise while yet you may,
For the debit side's increasing in a most alarming way;
The things you had no right to do,
the things you should have done,
They're all put down; it's up to you to pay for every one.
So eat, drink and be merry, have a good time if you will,
    But God help you when the time comes, and you
                              Foot the bill.

HOTEL

X305. Panoramic view of No. 16 Eldorado—
where Millionare Lippy of Seattle reaped his
harvest of gold—Y. T.

An intricate system of sluices surrounded the log cabins of the Klondike. During the spring thaw, these runways brought water from the surrounding hills, uncovering gold dust and nuggets.

The Shooting
of Dan McGrew

A bunch of the boys were whooping it up
    in the Malamute saloon;
The kid that handles the music-box
    was hitting a jag-time tune;
Back of the bar, in a solo game,
    sat Dangerous Dan McGrew,
And watching his luck was his light-o'-love,
    the lady that's known as Lou.

When out of the night, which was fifty below,
    and into the din and the glare,
There stumbled a miner fresh from the creeks,
    dog-dirty, and loaded for bear.
He looked like a man with a foot in the grave
    and scarcely the strength of a louse,
Yet he tilted a poke of dust on the bar,
    and he called for drinks for the house.
There was none could place the stranger's face,
    though we searched ourselves for a clue;
But we drank his health, and the last to drink
    was Dangerous Dan McGrew.

There's men that somehow just grip your eyes,
    and hold them hard like a spell;
And such was he, and he looked to me
    like a man who had lived in hell;
With a face most hair, and the dreary stare
    of a dog whose day is done,
As he watered the green stuff in his glass,
    and the drops fell one by one.
Then I got to figgering who he was,
    and wondering what he'd do,
And I turned my head—and there watching him
    was the lady that's known as Lou.

His eyes went rubbering round the room,
    and he seemed in a kind of daze,
Till at last that old piano fell
    in the way of his wandering gaze.
The ragtime kid was having a drink;
    there was no one else on the stool,
So the stranger stumbles across the room,
    and flops down there like a fool.
In a buckskin shirt that was glazed with dirt
    he sat, and I saw him sway;
Then he clutched the keys with his talon hands
    —my God, but that man could play!

Were you ever out in the Great Alone,
    when the moon was awful clear,
And the icy mountains hemmed you in
    with a silence you most could hear;
With only the howl of a timber wolf,
    and you camped there in the cold,
A half-dead thing in a stark, dead world,
    clean mad for the muck called gold;
While high overhead, green, yellow and red,
    the North Lights swept in bars?
Then you've a hunch what the music meant . . .
    hunger and night and the stars.

And hunger not of the belly kind
    that's banished with bacon and beans,
But the gnawing hunger of lonely men
    for a home and all that it means;
For a fireside far from the cares that are,
    four walls and a roof above;
But oh! so cramful of cozy joy,
    and crowned with a woman's love—

A woman dearer than all the world,
    and true as Heaven is true . . .
    (God! how ghastly she looks through her rouge—
    the lady that's known as Lou.)

Then on a sudden the music changed,
    so soft that you scarce could hear;
    But you felt that your life had been looted clean
    of all that it once held dear;
That someone had stolen the woman you loved;
    that her love was a devil's lie;
    That your guts were gone, and the best for you
    was to crawl away and die.
'Twas the crowning cry of a heart's despair,
    and it thrilled you through and through—
    "I guess I'll make it a spread misère,"
    said Dangerous Dan McGrew.

The music almost died away . . .
    then it burst like a pent-up flood;
    And it seemed to say, "Repay, repay,"
    and my eyes were blind with blood.
The thought came back of an ancient wrong,
    and it stung like a frozen lash,
    And the lust awoke to kill, to kill . . .
    then the music stopped with a crash,
And the stranger turned, and his eyes they burned
    in a most peculiar way;

In a buckskin shirt that was glazed with dirt
    he sat, and I saw him sway;
Then his lips went in in a kind of grin,
    and he spoke, and his voice was calm,
And "Boys," says he, "you don't know me,
    and none of you care a damn;
But I want to state, and my words are straight,
    and I'll bet my poke they're true,
That one of you is a hound of hell . . .
    and that one is Dan McGrew."

Then I ducked my head, and the lights went out,
    and two guns blazed in the dark,
And a woman screamed, and the lights went up,
    and two men lay stiff and stark.
Pitched on his head, and pumped full of lead,
    was Dangerous Dan McGrew,
While the man from the creeks lay clutched to the breast
    of the lady that's known as Lou.

These are the simple facts of the case,
    and I guess I ought to know.
    They say that the stranger was crazed with "hooch,"
    and I'm not denying it's so.
I'm not so wise as the lawyer guys,
    but strictly between us two
The woman that kissed him—and pinched his poke—
    was the lady that's known as Lou.

The Harpy

There was a woman, and she was wise; woefully wise was she;
She was old, so old, yet her years all told were but a score and three;
And she knew by heart, from finish to start, the Book of Iniquity.

There is no hope for such as I
    on earth, nor yet in Heaven;
  Unloved I live, unloved I die,
    unpitied, unforgiven;
A loathed jade, I ply my trade,
    unhallowed and unshriven.

I paint my cheeks, for they are white,
    and cheeks of chalk men hate;
  Mine eyes with wine I make to shine,
    that man may seek and sate;
With overhead a lamp of red
    I sit me down and wait.

Until they come, the nightly scum,
    with drunken eyes aflame;
  Your sweethearts, sons, ye scornful ones—
    It is I who know their shame.
The gods, ye see, are brutes to me—
    and so I play my game.

For life is not the thing we thought,
    and not the thing we plan;
  And Woman in a bitter world
    must do the best she can—
Must yield the stroke, and bear the yoke,
    and serve the will of man;

Must serve his need and ever feed
    the flame of his desire,
  Though be she loved for love alone,
    or be she loved for hire;
For every man since life began
    is tainted with the mire.

And though you know he love you so
    and set you on love's throne;
  Yet let your eyes but mock his sighs,
    and let your heart be stone,
Lest you be left (as I was left)
    attainted and alone.

From love's close kiss to hell's abyss
    is one sheer flight, I trow,
  And wedding ring and bridal bell
    are will-o'-wisps of woe,
And 'tis not wise to love too well,
    and this all women know.

Wherefore, the wolf-pack having gorged
    upon the lamb, their prey,
  With siren smile and serpent guile
    I make the wolf-pack pay—
With velvet paws and flensing claws,
    a tigress roused to slay.

One who in youth sought truest truth
　　and found a devil's lies;
A symbol of the sin of man,
　　a human sacrifice.
Yet shall I blame on man the shame?
　　Could it be otherwise?

Was I not born to walk in scorn
　　where others walk in pride?
The Maker marred, and, evil-starred,
　　I drift upon His tide;
And He alone shall judge His own,
　　so I His judgment bide.

Fate has written a tragedy, its name is "The Human Heart."
The Theatre is the House of Life, Woman the mummer's part;
The Devil enters the prompter's box, and the play is ready to start.

Loaded with supplies, this miner's mules are ready for a spring haul out to the claims.

The Ballad of the
Black Fox Skin

There was Claw-fingered Kitty and Windy Ike
    living the life of shame,
  When unto them in the Long, Long Night
    came the man-who-had-no-name;
Bearing his prize of a black fox pelt,
    out of the Wild he came.

His cheeks were blanched as the flume-head foam
    when the brown spring freshets flow;
  Deep in their dark, sin-calcined pits
    were his somber eyes aglow;
They knew him far for the fitful man
    who spat forth blood on the snow.

"Did ever you see such a skin?" quoth he,
    "there's nought in the world so fine—
Such fullness of fur as black as the night,
    such lustre, such size, such shine;
It's life to a one-lunged man like me;
    it's London, it's women, it's wine.

"The Moose-hides called it the devil-fox,
    and swore that no man could kill;
  That he who hunted it, soon or late,
    must surely suffer some ill;
But I laughed at them and their old squaw-tales.
    Ha! Ha! I'm laughing still.

"For look ye, the skin—it's as smooth as sin,
    and black as the core of the Pit.
  By gun or by trap, whatever the hap,
    I swore I would capture it;
By star and by star afield and afar,
    I hunted and would not quit.

"For the devil-fox, it was swift and sly,
    and it seemed to fleer at me;
  I would wake in fright by the camp-fire light,
    hearing its evil glee;
Into my dream its eyes would gleam,
    and its shadow would I see.

"It sniffed and ran from the ptarmigan
    I had poisoned to excess;
  Unharmed it sped from my wrathful lead
    ('twas as if I shot by guess);
Yet it came by night in the stark moonlight
    to mock at my weariness.

"I tracked it up where the mountains hunch
    like the vertebrae of the world;
  I tracked it down the death-still pits
    where the avalanche is hurled;
From the glooms to the sacerdotal snows,
    where the carded clouds are curled.

"From the vastitudes where the world protrudes
    through clouds like seas up-shoaled,
  I held its track till it led me back
    to the land I had left of old—
The land I had looted many moons.
    I was weary and sick and cold.

"I was sick, soul-sick, of the futile chase,
    and there and then I swore
  The foul fiend-fox might scathless go,
    for I would hunt no more;
Then I rubbed mine eyes in a vast surprise—
    it stood by my cabin door.

"A rifle raised in the wraith-like gloom,
    and a vengeful shot that sped;
  A howl that would thrill a cream-faced corpse—
    and the demon-fox lay dead . . .
Yet there was never a sign of wound,
    and never a drop he bled.
"So that was the end of the great black fox,
    and here is the prize I've won;
  And now for a drink to cheer me up—
    I've mushed since the early sun;
We'll drink a toast to the sorry ghost
    of the fox whose race is run."

II.

Now Claw-fingered Kitty and Windy Ike,
    bad as the worst were they.
  In their road-house down by the river-trail
    they waited and watched for prey;
With wine and song they joyed night long,
    and they slept like swine by day.

For things were done in the Midnight Sun
    that no tongue will ever tell;
  And men there be who walk earth-free,
    but whose names are writ in Hell—
Are writ in flames with the guilty names
    of Fournier and Labelle.

Put not your trust in a poke of dust
    would ye sleep the sleep of sin;
  For there be those who would rob your clothes
    ere yet the dawn comes in;
And a prize likewise in a woman's eyes
    is a peerless black fox skin.

Put your faith in the mountain cat
    if you lie within his lair;

Trust the fangs of the mother-wolf,
    and the claws of the lead-ripped bear;
But oh, of the wiles and the gold-tooth smiles
    of a dance-hall wench, beware!

Wherefore it was beyond all laws
    that lusts of man restrain,
  A man drank deep and sank to sleep
    never to wake again;
And the Yukon swallowed through a hole
    the cold corpse of the slain.

III.

The black fox skin a shadow cast
    from the roof nigh to the floor;
  And sleek it seemed and soft it gleamed,
    and the woman stroked it o'er;
And the man stood by with a brooding eye,
    and gnashed his teeth and swore.

When thieves and thugs fall out and fight
    there's fell arrears to pay;
  And soon or late sin meets its fate,
    and so it fell one day
That Claw-fingered Kitty and Windy Ike
    fanged up like dogs at bay.

"The skin is mine, all mine," she cried,
    "I did the deed alone."
  "It's share and share with a guilt-yoked pair,"
    he hissed in a pregnant tone;
And so they snarled like malamutes
    over a mildewed bone.

And so they fought, by fear untaught,
    till haply it befell
  One dawn of day she slipped away
    to Dawson town to sell

The fruit of sin, this black fox skin
    that had made their lives a hell.

She slipped away as still he lay,
    she clutched the wondrous fur.
Her pulses beat, her foot was fleet,
    her fear was as a spur;
She laughed with glee, she did not see
    him rise and follow her.

The bluffs uprear and grimly peer
    far over Dawson town;
They see its lights a blaze o' nights
    and harshly they look down;
They mock the plan and plot of man
    with grim, ironic frown.

The trail was steep; 'twas at the time
    when swiftly sinks the snow;
All honey-combed, the river ice
    was rotting down below;
The river chafed beneath its rind
    with many a mighty throe.

And up the swift and oozy drift
    a woman climbed in fear,
Clutching to her a black fox fur
    as if she held it dear;
And hard she pressed it to her breast—
    then Windy Ike drew near.

She made no moan—her heart was stone—
    she read his smiling face,
And like a dream flashed all her life's
    dark horror and disgrace;
A moment only—with a snarl
    he hurled her into space.

She rolled for nigh an hundred feet;
    she bounded like a ball;
From crag to crag she carromed down
    through snow and timber fall . . .
A hole gaped in the river ice;
    the spray flashed—that was all.

A bird sang for the joy of spring,
    so piercing sweet and frail;
And blinding bright the land was dight
    in gay and glittering mail;
And with a wondrous black fox skin
    a man slid down the trail.

IV.

A wedge-faced man there was who ran
    along the river bank,
Who stumbled through each drift and slough,
    and ever slipped and sank,
And ever cursed his Maker's name,
    and ever "hooch" he drank.

He travelled like a hunted thing,
    hard harried, sore distrest.
The old grandmother moon crept out
    from her cloud-quilted nest;
The aged mountains mocked at him
    in their primeval rest.

Grim shadows diapered the snow;
    the air was strangely mild;
The valley's girth was dumb with mirth,
    the laughter of the wild;
The still, sardonic laughter of
    an ogre o'er a child.

The river writhed beneath the ice;
    it groaned like one in pain,
And yawning chasms opened wide,
    and closed and yawned again;
And sheets of silver heaved on high
    until they split in twain.

From out the road-house by the trail
    they saw a man afar
Make for the narrow river-reach
    where the swift cross-currents are
Where, frail and worn, the ice is torn
    and the angry waters jar.

But they did not see him crash and sink
    into the icy flow;
They did not see him clinging here,

gripped by the undertow,
Clawing with bleeding fingernails
    at the jagged ice and snow.

They found a note beside the hole
    where he had stumbled in:
"Here met his fate by evil luck
    a man who lived in sin,
And to the one who loves me least
    I leave this black fox skin."

And strange it is; for, though they searched
    the river all around,
No trace or sign of black fox skin
    was ever after found;
Though one man said he saw the tread
    of hoofs deep in the ground.

Downtown Grand Forks at its peak—the second largest city north of Victoria and west of Winnipeg.

The Ballad of One-Eyed Mike

This is the tale that was told to me
by the man with the crystal eye,
As I smoked my pipe in the campfire light,
and the Glories swept the sky,
As the Northlights gleamed and curved and streamed,
and the bottle of "hooch" was dry.

A man once aimed that my life be shamed,
    and wrought me a deathly wrong,
I vowed one day I would well repay,
    but the heft of his hate was strong.
He thonged me East and he thonged me West;
    he harried me back and forth,
Till I fled in fright from his peerless spite
    to the bleak, bald-headed North.

And there I lay, and for many a day
    I hatched plan after plan,
For a golden haul of the wherewithal
    to crush and to kill my man;
And there I strove, and there I clove
    through the drift of icy streams;
And there I fought, and there I sought
    for the pay-streak of my dreams.

So twenty years, with their hopes and fears
    and smiles and tears and such,
Went by and left me long bereft
    of hope of the Midas touch;
About as fat as a chancel rat,
    and lo! despite my will,
In the weary fight I had clean lost sight
    of the man I sought to kill.

'Twas so far away, that evil day
    when I prayed the Prince of Gloom
For the savage strength and the sullen length
    of life to work his doom.
Nor sign nor word had I seen or heard,
    and it happed so long ago;
My youth was gone and my memory wan,
    and I willed it even so.

It fell one night in the waning light
    by the Yukon's oily flow,
I smoked and sat as I marvelled at
    the sky's port-winey glow;
Till it paled away to an absinthe gray,
    and the river seemed to shrink,
All wobbly flakes and wriggling snakes
    and goblin eyes a-wink.

'Twas weird to see and it 'wildered me
    in a queer, hypnotic dream,
Till I saw a spot like an inky blot
    come floating down the stream;
It bobbed and swung; it sheered and hung;
    it romped round in a ring;
It seemed to play in a tricksome way;
    it sure was a merry thing.

In freakish flights strange oily lights
    came fluttering round its head,
  Like butterflies of a monster size—
    then I knew it for the Dead.
Its face was rubbed and slicked and scrubbed
    as smooth as a shaven pate;
  In the silver snakes that the water makes
    it gleamed like a dinner-plate.

It gurgled near, and clear and clear
    and large and large it grew;
  It stood upright in a ring of light
    and it looked me through and through.
It weltered round with a woozy sound,
    and ere I could retreat,
  With the witless roll of a sodden soul
    it wantoned to my feet.

And here I swear by this Cross I wear,
    I heard that "floater" say:
  I am the man from whom you ran,
    the man you sought to slay.
That you may note and gaze and gloat,
    and say 'Revenge is sweet,'
  In the grit and grime of the river's slime
    I am rotting at your feet.

"The ill we rue we must e'en undo,
    though it rive us bone from bone;
  So it came about that I sought you out,

for I prayed I might atone.
I did you wrong, and for long and long
    I sought where you might live;
  And now you're found, though I'm dead and drowned,
    I beg you to forgive."

So sad it seemed and its cheek-bones gleamed,
    and its fingers flicked the shore;
  And it lapped and lay in a weary way,
    and its hands met to implore;
That I gently said: "Poor, restless dead,
    I would never work you woe;
  Though the wrong you rue you can ne'er undo
    I forgave you long ago."

Then, wonder-wise, I rubbed my eyes
    and I woke from a horrid dream.
  The moon rode high in the naked sky,
    and something bobbed in the stream.
It held my sight in a patch of light,
    and then it sheered from the shore;
  It dipped and sank by a hollow bank,
    and I never saw it more.

This was the tale be told to me,
    that man so warped and gray,
  Ere he slept and dreamed, and the camp-fire gleamed
    in his eye in a wolfish way—
That crystal eye that raked the sky
    in the weird Auroral ray.

Fresh meat was plentiful if miners wanted to take time to fish or hunt.

The Pines

We sleep in the sleep of ages,
    the bleak, barbarian pines;
  The gray moss drapes us like sages,
    and closer we lock our lines,
And deeper we clutch through the gelid gloom
    where never a sunbeam shines.

On the flanks of the storm-gored ridges
    are our black battalions massed;
  We surge in a host to the sullen coast,
    and we sing in the ocean blast;
From empire of sea to empire of snow
    we grip our empire fast.

To the niggard lands were we driven,
    'twixt desert and floes are we penned;
  To us was the Northland given,
    ours to stronghold and defend;
Ours till the world be riven
    in the crash of the utter end;

Ours from the bleak beginning,
    through the aeons of death-like sleep;
  Ours from the shock when the naked rock
    was hurled from the hissing deep;
Ours through the twilight ages
    of weary glacier creep.

Wind of the East, Wind of the West,
    wandering to and fro,
  Chant your songs in our topmost boughs,
    that the sons of men may know

The peerless pine was the first to come,
    and the pine will be last to go!

We pillar the halls of perfumed gloom;
    we plume where the eagles soar;
  The North-wind swoops from the brooding Pole,
    and our ancients crash and roar;
But where one falls from the crumbling walls
    shoots up a hardy score.

We spring from the gloom of the canyon's womb;
    in the valley's lap we lie;
  From the white foam-fringe, where the breakers cringe
    to the peaks that tusk the sky,
We climb, and we peer in the crag-locked mere
    that gleams like a golden eye.

Gain to the verge of the hog-back ridge
    where the vision ranges free:
  Pines and pines and the shadow of pines
    as far as the eye can see;
A steadfast legion of stalwart knights
    in dominant empery.

Sun, moon and stars give answer:
    shall we not staunchly stand
  Even as now, forever,
    wards of the wilder strand,
Sentinels of the stillness,
    lords of the last, lone land?

RECORD LOAD WOOD BONANZA 9 CORD

SPRING 1908

They seemed to measure everything in the Klondike in superlatives—and if it wasn't gold, how about a valuable load of wood? In the background is a rarity in the North, a huge angled window that provided much-needed light for the Kinseys' photography studio in Grand Forks.

The Wood-Cutter

The sky is like an envelope,
  One of those blue official things;
And, sealing it, to mock our hope,
  The moon, a silver wafer, clings.
What shall we find when death gives leave
  To read—our sentence or reprieve?

I'm holding it down on God's scrap-pile,
      up on the fag-end of earth;
  O'er me a menace of mountains,
      a river that grits at my feet;
Face to face with my soul-self,
      weighing my life at its worth;
  Wondering what I was made for,
      here in my last retreat.

Last! Ah, yes, it's the finish.
      Have ever you heard a man cry?
  (Sobs that rake him and rend him,
      right from the base of the chest.)
That's how I've cried, oh, so often;
      and now that my tears are dry,
  I sit in the desolate quiet
      and wait for the infinite Rest.

Rest! Well, it's restful around me;
      it's quiet clean to the core.
  The mountains pose in their ermine,
      in golden the hills are clad;
The big, blue, silt-freighted Yukon
      seethes by my cabin door,
  And I think it's only the river
      that keeps me from going mad.

By day it's a ruthless monster,
  a callous, insatiate thing,
 With oily bubble and eddy,
  with sudden swirling of breast;
By night it's a writhing Titan,
  sullenly murmuring,
 Ever and ever goaded,
  and ever crying for rest.

It cries for its human tribute,
  but me it will never drown.
I've learned the lore of my river;
  my river obeys me well.
I hew and I launch my cordwood,
  and raft it to Dawson town,
Where wood means wine and women,
  and, incidentally, Hell.

Hell and the anguish thereafter.
  Here as I sit alone
I'd give the life I have left me
  to lighten some load of care:
(The bitterest part of the bitter
  is being denied to atone;
Lips that have mocked at Heaven
  lend themselves ill to prayer.)

Impotent as a beetle pierced on the needle of Fate;
 A wretch in a cosmic death-cell,
 peaks for my prison bars;
'Whelmed by a world stupendous,
 lonely and listless I wait,
 Drowned in a sea of silence,
  strewn with confetti of stars.

See! from far up the valley
  a rapier pierces the night,
 The white search-ray of a steamer.
  Swiftly, serenely it nears;
A proud, white, alien presence,
  a glittering galley of light,
 Confident—poised, triumphant,
  freighted with hopes and fears.
I look as one looks on a vision;
  I see it pulsating by;
 I glimpse joy-radiant faces;
  I hear the thresh of the wheel.
Hoof-like my heart beats a moment;
  then silence swoops from the sky.
 Darkness is piled upon darkness.
  God only knows how I feel.

Maybe you've seen me sometimes
  maybe you've pitied me then—
 The lonely waif of the wood-camp,
  here by my cabin door.
Some day you'll look and see not;
  futile and outcast of men,
 I shall be far from your pity,
  resting forevermore.

My life was a problem in ciphers,
 a weary and profitless sum.
 Slipshod and stupid I worked it,
  dazed by negation and doubt.
Ciphers the total confronts me.
 Oh, Death, with thy moistened thumb,
 Stoop like a petulant schoolboy,
  wipe me forever out!

The Telegraph Operator

I will not wash my face;
    I will not brush my hair;
I "pig" around the place—
    There's nobody to care.
Nothing but rock and tree;
    Nothing but wood and stone,
Oh, God, it's hell to be
    Alone, alone, alone!

Snow-peaks and deep-gashed draws
    Corral me in a ring.
I feel as if I was
    The only living thing
On all this blighted earth;
    And so I frowst and shrink,
And crouching by my hearth
    I hear the thoughts I think.

I think of all I miss—
    The boys I used to know;
The girls I used to kiss;
    The coin I used to blow;
The bars I used to haunt;
    The racket and the row;
The beers I didn't want
    (I wish I had 'em now).

Day after day the same,
    Only a little worse;
No one to grouch or blame—
    Oh, for a loving curse!
Oh, in the night I fear,
    Haunted by nameless things,
Just for a voice to cheer,
    Just for a hand that clings!

Faintly as from a star
    Voices come o'er the line;
Voices of ghosts afar,
    Not in this world of mine;
Lives in whose loom I grope;
    Words in whose weft I hear
Eager the thrill of hope,
    Awful the chill of fear.

I'm thinking out aloud;
    I reckon that is bad;
(The snow is like a shroud)—
    Maybe I'm going mad.
Say! wouldn't that be tough?
    This awful hush that hugs
And chokes one is enough
    To make a man go "bugs."

There's not a thing to do;
    I cannot sleep at night;
No wonder I'm so blue;
    Oh, for a friendly fight!
The din and rush of strife;
    A music-hall aglow;
A crowd, a city, life—
    Dear God, I miss it so!

Here, you have moped enough
    Brace up and play the game!
But say, it's awful tough—
    Day after day the same
(I've said that twice, I bet).
    Well, there's not much to say.
I wish I had a pet,
    Or something I could play.

Cheer up! don't get so glum
    And sick of everything.
The worst is yet to come;
    God help you till the Spring.
God shield you from the Fear;
    Teach you to laugh, not moan.
Ha! ha! it sounds so queer—
    Alone, alone, alone!

PERCENTAGE AVENUE, GRAND FORKS

Grand Forks, the small town 14 miles from the roaring city of Dawson, was home to some 10,000 miners and their families. During the spring thaw, the streets became muddy quagmires.

The first winter after the discovery of gold, sturdy cabins were
already the norm and temporary tent cities had all but disappeared.

The Ballad of
Pious Pete

"The North has got him."—Yukonism.

I tried to refine that neighbor of mine,
    honest to God, I did.
  I grieved for his fate, and early and late
    I watched over him like a kid.
I gave him excuse, I bore his abuse
    in every way that I could.
  I swore to prevail; I camped on his trail;
    I plotted and planned for his good.
By day and by night I strove in men's sight
    to gather him into the fold,
  With precept and prayer, with hope and despair,
    in hunger and hardship and cold.
I followed him into Gehennas of sin,
    I sat where the sirens sit;
  In the shade of the Pole, for the sake of his soul,
    I strove with the powers of the Pit.
I shadowed him down to the scrofulous town;
    I dragged him from dissolute brawls;
  But I killed the galoot when he started to shoot
    electricity into my walls.

God knows what I did, that he'd seek to be rid
    of one who would save him from shame.
  God knows what I bore that night when he swore
    and bade me make tracks from his claim.
I started to tell of the horrors of Hell,
    when sudden his eyes lit like coals;
  And "Chuck it," says he, "don't persecute me
    with your cant and your saving of souls."

I'll swear I was mild as I'd be with a child,
    but he called me the son of a slut;
  And, grabbing his gun with a leap and a run,
    he threatened my face with the butt.

So what could I do (I leave it to you)?
        With curses he harried me forth;
    Then he was alone, and I was alone,
        and over us menaced the North.

Our cabins were near; I could see, I could hear;
        but between us there rippled the creek;
    And all summer through, with a rancor that grew,
        he would pass me and never would speak.
Then a shuddery breath like the coming of Death
        crept down from the peaks far away.
    The water was still; the twilight was chill;
        the sky was a tatter of gray.
Swift came the Big Cold, and opal and gold
        the lights of the witches arose;
    The frost-tyrant clinched, and the valley was cinched
        by the stark and cadaverous snows.
The trees were like lace where the star-beams could chase,
        each leaf was a jewel agleam.
    The soft white hush lapped the Northland and wrapped
        us round in a crystalline dream;
So still I could hear quite loud in my ear
        the swish of the pinions of time;
    So bright I could see, as plain as could be,
        the wings of God's angels ashine.

As I read in the Book I would oftentimes look
        to that cabin just over the creek.
    Ah me, it was sad and evil and bad,
        two neighbors who never would speak!
I knew that full well like a devil in Hell
        he was hatching out, early and late,
    A system to bear through the frost-spangled air
        the warm, crimson waves of his hate.
I only could peer and shudder and fear,
        'twas ever so ghastly and still;
    But I knew over there in his lonely despair
        he was plotting me terrible ill.
I knew that he nursed a malice accurst,
        like the blast of a winnowing flame;

I pleaded aloud for a shield, for a shroud
    Oh, God! then calamity came.

Mad? If I'm mad, then you too are mad;
    but it's all in the point of view.
If you'd look at them things gallivantin' on wings,
    all purple and green and blue;
If you'd noticed them twist, as they mounted and hissed
    like scorpions dim in the dark;
If you'd seen them rebound with a horrible sound,
    and spitefully spitting a spark;
If you'd watched *It* with dread, as it hissed by your bed,
    that thing with the feelers that crawls
You'd have settled the brute that attempted to shoot
    electricity into your walls.

Oh, some, they were blue, and they slithered right through;
    they were silent and squashy and round;
And some, they were green; they were wriggly and lean;
    they writhed with so hateful a sound.
My blood seemed to freeze; I fell on my knees;
    my face was a white splash of dread.
Oh, the Green and the Blue, they were gruesome to view;
    but the worst of them all were the Red.
They came through the door, they came through the floor,
    they came through the moss-creviced logs.
They were savage and dire; they were whiskered with fire;
    they bickered like malamute dogs.
They ravined in rings like iniquitous things;
    they gulped down the Green and the Blue.
I crinkled with fear whene'er they drew near,
    and nearer and nearer they drew.

And then came the crown of Horror's grim crown,
    the monster so loathsomely red.
Each eye was a pin that shot out and in,
    as, squid-like, it oozed to my bed.
So softly it crept with feelers that swept
    and quivered like fine copper wire;

Its belly was white with a sulphurous light,
    its jaws were a-drooling with fire.
It came and it came; I could breathe of its flame,
    but never a wink could I look.
I thrust in its maw the Fount of the Law;
    I fended it off with the Book.
I was weak—oh, so weak—but I thrilled at its shriek,
    as wildly it fled in the night;
And deathlike I lay till the dawn of the day.
    (Was ever so welcome the light?)

I loaded my gun at the rise of the sun;
    to his cabin so softly I stunk.
My neighbor was there in the frost-freighted air,
    all wrapped in a robe in his bunk.
It muffled his moans; it outlined his bones,
    as feebly he twisted about;
His gums were so black, and his lips seemed to crack,
    and his teeth all were loosening out.
'Twas a death's head that peered through the tangle of beard;
    'twas a face I will never forget;
Sunk eyes full of woe, and they troubled me so
    with their pleadings and anguish; and yet
As I rested my gaze in a misty amaze
    on the scurvy-degenerate wreck,
I thought of the Things with the dragon-fly wings,
    then laid I my gun on his neck.
He gave out a cry that was faint as a sigh,
    like a perishing malamute,
And he says unto me, "I'm converted," says he;
    "for Christ's sake, Peter, don't shoot!"

They're taking me out with an escort about,
    and under a sergeant's care;
I am humbled indeed, for I'm 'cuffed to a Swede
    who thinks he's a millionaire.
But it's all Gospel true what I'm telling to you
    up there where the Shadow falls
That I settled Sam Noot when he started to shoot
    electricity into my walls.

The Lone Trail

Ye who know the Lone Trail fain would follow it,
Though it lead to glory or the darkness of the pit.
Ye who take the Lone Trail, bid your love goodbye;
The Lone Trail, the Lone Trail follow till you die.

The trails of the world be countless,
    and most of the trails be tried;
  You tread on the heels of the many,
    till you come where the ways divide;
And one lies safe in the sunlight,
    and the other is dreary and wan,
  Yet you look aslant at the Lone Trail,
    and the Lone Trail lures you on.
And somehow you're sick of the highway,
    with its noise and its easy needs,
  And you seek the risk of the by-way,
    and you reck not where it leads.
And sometimes it leads to the desert,
    and the tongue swells out of the mouth,
  And you stagger blind to the mirage,
    to die in the mocking drouth.
And sometimes it leads to the mountain,
    to the light of the lone camp-fire,
  And you gnaw your belt in the anguish
    of hunger-goaded desire.
And sometimes it leads to the Southland,

    to the swamp where the orchid glows,
  And you rave to your grave with the fever,
    and they rob the corpse for its clothes.
And sometimes it leads to the Northland,
    and the scurvy softens your bones,
  And your flesh dints in like putty,
    and you spit out your teeth like stones.
And sometimes it leads to a coral reef
    in the wash of a weedy sea,
  And you sit and stare at the empty glare
    where the gulls wait greedily.
And sometimes it leads to an Arctic trail,
    and the snows where your torn feet freeze,
  And you whittle away the useless clay,
    and crawl on your hands and knees.
Often it leads to the dead-pit;
    always it leads to pain;
  By the bones of your brothers ye know it,
    but oh, to follow you're fain.
By your bones they will follow behind you,
    till the ways of the world are made plain.

Bid goodbye to sweetheart, bid goodbye to friend;
The Lone Trail, the Lone Trail follow to the end.
Tarry not, and fear not, chosen of the true;
Lover of The Lone Trail, The Lone Trail waits for you.

NO 4 BELOW ON BONANZA

The back-breaking labor of mining became slightly easier when the ore car was introduced to mining claims.

The Song of the Wage-Slave

When the long, long day is over,
    and the Big Boss gives me my pay,
I hope that it won't be hell-fire,
    as some of the parsons say.
And I hope that it won't be heaven,
    with some of the parsons I've met—
All I want is just quiet, just to rest and forget.
Look at my face, toil-furrowed;
    look at my calloused hands;
Master, I've done Thy bidding,
    wrought in Thy many lands—
Wrought for the little masters,
    big-bellied they be, and rich;
I've done their desire for a daily hire,
    and I die like a dog in a ditch.
I have used the strength Thou hast given,
    Thou knowest I did not shirk;
Threescore years of labor—
    Thine be the long day's work.
And now, Big Master, I'm broken
    and bent and twisted and scarred,
But I've held my job, and Thou knowest,
    and Thou wilt not judge me hard.

Thou knowest my sins are many,
    and often I've played the fool
Whiskey and cards and women,
    they made me the devil's tool.
I was just like a child with money
    I flung it away with a curse,
Feasting a fawning parasite,
    or glutting a harlot's purse;

Then back to the woods repentant,
    back to the mill or the mine,
I, the worker of workers,
    everything in my line.
Everything hard but headwork
    (I'd no more brains than a kid),
A brute with brute strength to labor,
    doing as I was bid;
Living in camps with men-folk,
    a lonely and loveless life;
Never knew kiss of sweetheart,
    never caress of wife.
A brute with brute strength to labor,
    and they were so far above
Yet I'd gladly have gone to the gallows
    for one little look of Love.
I, with the strength of two men,
    savage and shy and wild
Yet how I'd ha' treasured a woman,
    and the sweet, warm kiss of a child!

Well, 'tis Thy world, and Thou knowest.
    I blaspheme and my ways be rude;
But I've lived my life as I found it,
    and I've done my best to be good;
I, the primitive toiler,
    half-naked and grimed to the eyes,
Sweating it deep in their ditches,
    swining it stark in their styes;
Hurling down forests before me,
    spanning tumultuous streams;
Down in the ditch building o'er me
    palaces fairer than dreams;

Boring the rock to the ore-bed,
            driving the road through the fen,
Resolute, dumb, uncomplaining,
            a man in a world of men.
Master, I've filled my contract,
            wrought in Thy many lands;
Not by my sins wilt Thou judge me,
            but by the work of my hands.
Master, I've done Thy bidding,
            and the light is low in the west,
And the long, long shift is over . . .
            Master, I've earned it—Rest.

In the spring and summer months, mine owners and hourly laborers worked almost around the clock.

The Prospector

I strolled up old Bonanza,
      where I staked in 'Ninety-Eight,
  A-purpose to revisit the old claim.
I kept thinking mighty sadly
      of the funny ways of Fate,
  And the lads who once were with me in the game.
Poor boys, they're down-and-outers,
      and there's scarcely one to-day
  Can show a dozen colors in his poke;
And me, I'm still prospecting,
      old and battered, gaunt and gray,
  And I'm looking for a grubstake, and I'm broke.

I strolled up old Bonanza.
      The same old moon looked down;
  The same old landmarks seemed to yearn to me;
But the cabins all were silent,
      and the flat, once like a town,
  Was mighty still and lonesome-like to see.
There were piles and piles of tailings
      where we toiled with pick and pan,
  And turning round a bend I heard a roar,
And there a giant gold-ship
      of the very newest plan
  Was tearing chunks of pay-dirt from the shore.

It wallowed in its water-bed;
      it burrowed, heaved and swung;
  It gnawed its way ahead with grunts and sighs;
Its bill of fare was rock and sand;
      the tailings were its dung;
  It glared around with fierce electric eyes.
Full fifty buckets crammed its maw;
      it bellowed out for more;
  It looked like some great monster in the gloom.

With two to feed its sateless greed,
      it worked for seven score,
  And I sighed: "Ah, old-time miner, here's your doom!"
The idle windlass turns to rust;
      the sagging sluice-box falls;
  The holes you digged are water to the brim.
Your little sod-roofed cabins
      with the snugly moss-chinked walls
  Are deathly now and mouldering and dim.
The battlefield is silent where
      of old you fought it out;
  The claims you fiercely won are lost and sold;
But there's a little army
      that they'll never put to rout
  The men who simply live to seek the gold.

The men who can't remember
      when they learned to swing a pack,
  Or in what lawless land the quest began;
The solitary seeker
      with his grubstake on his back,
  The restless buccaneer of pick and pan.
On the mesas of the Southland,
      on the tundras of the North,
  You will find us, changed in face but still the same;
And it isn't need, it isn't greed
      that sends us faring forth
  It's the fever, it's the glory of the game.

For once you've panned the speckled sand
      and seen the bonny dust,
  Its peerless brightness blinds you like a spell;
It's little else you care about;
      you go because you must,
  And you feel that you could follow it to Hell.

You'd follow it in hunger,
  and you'd follow it in cold;
 You'd follow it in solitude and pain;
And when you're stiff and battened down,
  let someone whisper "Gold,"
 You're lief to rise and follow it again.

Yet look you, if I find the stuff
  it's just like so much dirt;
 I fling it to the four winds like a child.
It's wine and painted women
  and the things that do me hurt,
 Till I crawl back, beggared, broken, to the Wild.
Till I crawl back, sapped and sodden,
  to my grubstake and my tent
 There's a city, there's an army (hear them shout).
There's the gold in millions, millions,
  but I haven't got a cent;
 And oh, it's me, it's me that found it out.

It was my dream that made it good,
  my dream that made me go
 To the lands of dread and death disprized of man;
But oh, I've known a glory
  that their hearts will never know,
 When I picked the first big nugget from my pan.
It's still my dream, my dauntless dream,
  that drives me forth once more
 To seek and starve and suffer in the Vast;
That heaps my heart with eager hope,
  that glimmers on before
 My dream that will uplift me to the last.

Perhaps I am stark crazy, but
  there's none of you too sane;
 It's just a little matter of degree.
My hobby is to hunt our gold;
  it's fortressed in my brain;
 It's life and love and wife and home to me.
And I'll strike it, yes, I'll strike it;
  I've a hunch I cannot fail;
 I've a vision, I've a prompting, I've a call;
I hear the hoarse stampeding
  of an army on my trail,
 To the last, the greatest gold camp of them all.

Beyond the shark-tooth ranges
  sawing savage at the sky
 There's a lowering land no white man ever struck.
There's gold, there's gold in millions,
  and I'll find it if I die,
 And I'm going there once more to try my luck.
Maybe I'll fail—what matter?
  It's a mandate, it's a vow;
 And when in lands of dreariness and dread
  You seek the last lone frontier,
 far beyond your frontiers now,
You will find the old prospector, silent, dead.

You will find a tattered tent-pole
  with a raged robe below it;
 You'll find a rusted gold-pan on the sod;
You will find the claim I'm seeking,
  with my bones as stakes to show it;
 But I've sought the last Recorder, and He's—God.

Miners would thaw a column of frozen ground and dig, thaw, and dig all winter. Come spring, they would shovel the gold-bearing rock and gravel through the sluices and hope that the ground held a rich vein.

The rocker box or jigger was used to wash out the fine gold dust so that it wouldn't disappear through the cruder sluices.

My Friends

The man above was a murderer,
    the man below was a thief;
  And I lay there in the bunk between,
    ailing beyond belief;
A weary armful of skin and bone,
    wasted with pain and grief.

My feet were froze, and the lifeless toes
    were purple and green and gray.
  The little flesh that clung to my bones,
    you could punch in it holes like clay;
The skin on my gums was a sullen black,
    and slowly peeling away.

I was sure enough in a direful fix,
    and often I wondered why
  They did not take the chance that was left
    and leave me alone to die,
Or finish me off with a dose of dope
    so utterly lost was I.

But no; they brewed me the green-spruce tea,
    and nursed me there like a child;
  And the homicide, he was good to me,
    and bathed my sores and smiled;
And the thief, he starved that I might be fed,
    and his eyes were kind and mild.

Yet they were woefully wicked men,
    and often at night in pain
  I heard the murderer speak of his deed
    and dream it—over again;
I heard the poor thief sorrowing for
    the dead self he had slain.

I'll never forget that bitter dawn,
    so evil, askew and gray,
  When they wrapped me round in the skins of beasts
    and they bore me to a sleigh,
And we started out with the nearest post
    an hundred miles away.

I'll never forget the trail they broke,
    with its tense, unuttered woe;
  And the crunch, crunch, crunch as their showshoes sank
    through the crust of the hollow snow;
And my breath would fail, and every beat
    of my heart was like a blow.

And oftentimes I would die the death,
    yet wake up to life anew;
  The sun would be all ablaze on the waste,
    and the sky a blighting blue,
And the tears would rise in my snow-blind eyes
    and furrow my cheeks like dew.

And the camps we made when their strength outplayed
    and the day was pinched and wan;
  And oh, the joy of that blessed halt,
    and how I did dread the dawn;
And how I hated the weary men
    who rose and dragged me on.

And oh, how I begged to rest, to rest
    the snow was so sweet a shroud!
  And oh, how I cried when they urged me on,
    cried and cursed them aloud!
Yet on they strained, all racked and pained,
    and sorely their backs were bowed.

And then it was all like a lurid dream,
    and I prayed for a swift release
From the ruthless ones who would not leave
    me to die alone in peace;
Till I wakened up and I found myself
    at the post of the Mounted Police.

And there was my friend the murderer,
    and there was my friend the thief,
With bracelets of steel around their wrists,
    and wicked beyond belief:
But when they come to God's judgment seat
    may I be allowed the brief.

The Kinseys took their cameras and enthusiasm west when gold was discovered on the beaches of Nome, Alaska, but the Klondike was their real love—and their home well after the glory years of the gold rush.

KINSEY&KINSEY.PHTO.Y.T.

Robertson & Co., Grand Forks Stag

The stages ran often along the Klondike trails, but "often" in Klondike terms meant a wait as long as several hours. Most Klondikers had no patience—they loaded the stages as full as their owners—and the horse teams—would allow.

The Black Sheep

"In Canada, the aristocratic ne'er-do-well frequently finds his way into
the ranks of the Royal Northwest Mounted Police."—Extract.

Hark to the ewe that bore him:
"What has muddied the strain?
Never his brothers before him
Showed the hint of a stain."
Hark to the tups and wethers;
Hark to the old gray ram:
"We're all of us white, but he's black as night,
And he'll never be worth a damn."

I'm up on the bally wood-pile
at the back of the barracks yard;
"A damned disgrace to the force, sir,"
with a comrade standing guard;
Making the bluff I'm busy,
doing my six months hard.

"Six months hard and dismissed, sir."
Isn't that rather hell?
And all because of the liquor laws
and the wiles of a native belle
Some "hooch" I gave to a Siwash brave
who swore that he wouldn't tell.

At least they say that I did it.
It's so in the town report.
All that I can recall is
a night of revel and sport,
When I woke with a "head" in the guardroom,
and they dragged me sick into court.

And the O.C. said: "You are guilty,"
    and I said never a word;
  For, hang it, you see I couldn't—
    didn't know what had occurred,
And, under the circumstances,
    denial would be absurd.

But the one that cooked my bacon
    was Grubbe, of the City Patrol.
  He fagged for my room at Eton,
    and didn't I devil his soul!
And now he is getting even,
    landing me down in the hole.

Plugging away on the wood-pile;
    doing chores around the square.
  There goes an officer's lady
    gives me a haughty stare.
Me that's an earl's own nephew
    that is the hardest to bear.

To think of the poor old mater
    awaiting her prodigal son.
  Tho' I broke her heart with my folly,
    I was always the white-haired one.
(That fatted calf that they're cooking
    will surely be overdone.)

I'll go back and yarn to the Bishop;
    I'll dance with the village belle;
I'll hand round tea to the ladies,
    and everything will be well.
Where I have been won't matter;
    what I have seen I won't tell.

I'll soar to their ken like a comet.
    They'll see me with never a stain
But will they reform me?—far from it.

We pay for our pleasure with pain;
But the dog will return to his vomit,
    the hog to his wallow again.

I've chewed on the rind of creation,
    and bitter I've tasted the same.
  Stacked up against hell and damnation,
    I've managed to stay in the game.
I've had my moments of sorrow;
    I've had my seasons of shame.

That's past; when one's nature's a cracked one,
    it's too jolly hard to mend.
  So long as the road is level,
    so long as I've cash to spend,
I'm bound to go to the devil,
    and it's all the same in the end.

The bugle is sounding for stables;
    the men troop off through the gloom;
  An orderly laying the tables
    sings in the bright mess-room.
(I'll wash in the prison bucket,
    and brush with the prison broom.)

I'll lie in my cell and listen;
    I'll wish that I couldn't hear
The laugh and the chaff of the fellows
    swigging the canteen beer;
The nasal tone of the gramophone
    playing "The Bandolier."

And it seems to me, though it's misty,
    that night of the flowing bowl,
  That the man who potlatched the whiskey
    and landed me into the hole
Was Grubbe, that unmerciful bounder—
    Grubbe, of the City Patrol.

Gold dust fills the cleanup sluice box, as miners, their wives and laborers gather for the sweep-up and weigh-in.

Clancy of The Mounted Police

In the little Crimson Manual
    it's written plain and clear
  That who would wear the scarlet coat
    shall say good-bye to fear;
Shall be a guardian of the right,
    a sleuth-hound of the trail
  In the little Crimson Manual
    there's no such word as "fail"
Shall follow on, though heavens fall,
    or Hell's top-turrets freeze,
  Half round the world, if need there be,
    on bleeding hands and knees.

It's duty, duty, first and last,
    the Crimson Manual saith;
  The Scarlet Riders make reply:
    "it's duty—to the death."
And so they sweep the solitudes,
    free men from all the earth;
  And so they sentinel the woods,
    the wilds that know their worth;
And so they scour the startled plains
    and mock at hurt and pain,
  And read their Crimson Manual,
    and find their duty plain.

Knights of the lists of unrenown,
    born of the frontier's need,
  Disdainful of the spoken word,
    exultant in the deed;
Unconscious heroes of the waste,
    proud players of the game,
  Props of the power behind the throne,
    upholders of the name;
For thus the Great White Chief hath said:
    "In all my lands be peace,"

And to maintain his word he gave
    his West the Scarlet Police.

Livid-lipped was the valley,
    still as the grave of God;
  Misty shadows of mountain
    thinned into mists of cloud;
Corpselike and stark was the land,
    with a quiet that crushed and awed,
  And the stars of the weird sub-arctic
    glimmered over its shroud.
Deep in the trench of the valley
    two men stationed the Post,
  Seymour and Clancy the reckless,
    fresh from the long patrol;
Seymour, the sergeant, and Clancy—
    Clancy who made his boast
  He could cinch like a bronco the Northland,
    and cling to the prongs of the Pole.

Two lone men on detachment,
    standing for law on the trail;
  Undismayed in the vastness,
    wise with the wisdom of old
Out of the night hailed a half-breed
    telling a pitiful tale:
  "White man starving and crazy
    on the banks of the Nordenscold."
Up sprang the red-haired Clancy,
    lean and eager of eye;
  Loaded the long toboggan,
    strapped each dog at its post;
Whirled his lash at the leader;
    then, with a whoop and a cry,
  Into the Great White Silence
    faded away like a ghost.

The clouds were a misty shadow,
      the hills were a shadowy mist;
  Sunless, voiceless and pulseless,
      the day was a dream of woe;
Through the ice-rifts the river smoked
      and bubbled and hissed;
  Behind was a trail fresh broken,
      in front the untrodden snow.

Ahead of the dogs ploughed Clancy,
      haloed by steaming breath;
  Through peril of open water,
      through ache of insensate cold;
Up rivers wantonly winding
      in a land affianced to death,
  Till he came to a cowering cabin
      on the banks of the Nordenscold.
Then Clancy loosed his revolver,
      and he strode through the open door;
  And there was the man he sought for,
      crouching beside the fire;
The hair of his beard was singeing,
      the frost on his back was hoar,
  And ever he crooned and chanted
      as if he never would tire:—

"I panned and I panned in the shiny sand,
      and I sniped on the river bar;
  But I know, I know, that it's down
      below that the golden treasures are;
So I'll wait and wait till the floods abate,
      and I'll sink a shaft once more,
  And I'd like to bet that I'll go home yet
      with a brass-band playing before."

He was nigh as thin as a sliver,
      and he whined like a Moose-hide cur;
  So Clancy clothed him and nursed him
      as a mother nurses a child;

Lifted him on the toboggan,
      wrapped him in robes of fur,
  Then with the dogs sore straining
      started to face the Wild.

Said the Wild, "I will crush this Clancy,
      so fearless and insolent;
  For him will I loose my fury,
      and blind and buffet and beat;
Pile up my snows to stay him;
      then when his strength is spent,
  Leap on him from my ambush
      and crush him under my feet.

"Him will I ring with my silence,
      compass him with my cold;
  Closer and closer clutch him
      unto mine icy breast;
Buffet him with my blizzards,
      deep in my snows enfold,
  Claiming his life as my tribute,
      giving my wolves the rest."

Clancy crawled through the vastness;
      o'er him the hate of the Wild;
  Full on his face fell the blizzard;
      cheering his huskies he ran;
Fighting, fierce-hearted and tireless,
      snows that drifted and piled,
  With ever and ever behind him
      singing the crazy man:

"Sing hey, sing ho, for the ice and snow,
    And a heart that's ever merry,
Let us trim and square with a lover's care
    —For why should a man be sorry?—
A grave deep, deep, with the moon a-peep,
    A grave in the frozen mold.
Sing hey, sing ho, for the winds that blow,

And a grave deep down in the ice and snow,
  A grave in the land of gold.”

Day after day of darkness,
    the whirl of the seething snows;
  Day after day of blindness,
    the swoop of the stinging blast;
On through a blur of fury
    the swing of staggering blows;
  On through a world of turmoil,
    empty, inane and vast.

Night with its writhing storm-whirl,
    night despairingly black;
  Night with its hours of terror,
    numb and endlessly long;
Night with its weary waiting,
    fighting the shadows back,
  And ever the crouching madman
    singing his crazy song.

Cold with its creeping terror,
    cold with its sudden clinch;
  Cold so utter you wonder
    if ’twill ever again be warm;
Clancy grinned as he shuddered,
    “Surely it isn’t a cinch
  Being wet-nurse to a looney
    in the teeth of an arctic storm.”

The blizzard passed and the dawn broke,
    knife-edged and crystal clear;
  The sky was a blue-domed iceberg,
    sunshine outlawed away;
Ever by snowslide and ice-rip
    haunted and hovered the Fear;
  Ever the Wild malignant
    poised and panted to slay.

The lead-dog freezes in harness—
    cut him out of the team!
  The lung of the wheel-dog’s bleeding—
    shoot him and let him lie!
On and on with the others—
    slash them until they scream!
  “Pull for your lives, you devils!
    On! To halt is to die.”

There in the frozen vastness
    Clancy fought with his foes;
  The ache of the stiffened fingers,
    the cut of the snowshoe thong;
Cheeks black-raw through the hood-flap,
    eyes that tingled and closed,
  And ever to urge and cheer him
    quavered the madman’s song.

Colder it grew and colder,
    till the last heat left the earth,
  And there in the great stark stillness
    the bale fires glinted and gleamed,
And the Wild all around exulted
    and shook with a devilish mirth,
  And life was far and forgotten,
    the ghost of a joy once dreamed.

Death! And one who defied it,
    a man of the Mounted Police;
  Fought it there to a standstill
    long after hope was gone;
Grinned through his bitter anguish,
    fought without let or cease,
  Suffering, straining, striving,
    stumbling, struggling on,

Till the dogs lay down in their traces,
    and rose and staggered and fell;

Till the eyes of him dimmed with shadows,
    and the trail was so hard to see;
Till the Wild howled out triumphant,
    and the world was a frozen hell
Then said Constable Clancy:
    "I guess that it's up to me."

Far down the trail they saw him,
    and his hands, they were blanched like bone;
His face was a blackened horror,
    from his eye-lids the salt rheum ran.
His feet he was lifting strangely,
    as if they were made of stone,
But safe in his arms and sleeping
    he carried the crazy man.

So Clancy got into Barracks,
    and the boys made rather a scene;
And the O.C. called him a hero,
    and was nice as a man could be;
But Clancy gazed down his trousers
    at the place where his toes had been,
And then he howled like a husky,
    and sang in a shaky key:

"When I go back to the old love
    that's true to the finger-tips,
I'll say: 'Here's bushels of gold, love,'
    and I'll kiss my girl on the lips;
'It's yours to have and to hold, love.'
    It's the proud, proud boy I'll be,
When I go back to the old love
    that's waited so long for me."

The Royal Canadian Mounted Police were the peacekeepers, jailers, mail carriers, tax collectors, and good friends to those who lived in the northern territories.

Always dapper, photographer Clarke Kinsey and his wife, Mary, pose outside their Grand Forks cabin.

Music in the Bush

O'er the dark pines she sees the silver moon,
    And in the west, all tremulous, a star;
And soothing sweet she hears the mellow tune
    Of cow-bells jangled in the fields afar.

Quite listless, for her daily stent is done,
    She stands, sad exile, at her rose-wreathed door,
And sends her love eternal with the sun
    That goes to gild the land she'll see no more.

The grave, gaunt pines imprison her sad gaze,
    All still the sky and darkling drearily;
She feels the chilly breath of dear, dead days
    Come sifting through the alders eerily.

Oh, how the roses riot in their bloom!
    The curtains stir as with an ancient pain.
Her old piano gleams from out the gloom
    And waits and waits her tender touch in vain.

But now her hands like moonlight brush the keys
    With velvet grace-melodious delight;
And now a sad refrain from over seas
    Goes sobbing on the bosom of the night;

And now she sings (Oh singer in the gloom,
    Voicing a sorrow we can ne'er express,
Here in the Fatness where we few have room
    Unshamed to show our love and tenderness,

Our hearts will echo, till they beat no more,
    That song of sadness and of motherland;

And, stretched in deathless love to England's shore,
    Some day she'll hearken and she'll understand.)

A prima-donna in the shining past,
    But now a mother growing old and gray,
She thinks of how she held a people fast
    In thrall, and gleaned the triumphs of a day.

She sees a sea of faces like a dream;
    She sees herself a queen of song once more;
She sees lips part in rapture, eyes agleam;
    She sings as never once she sang before.

She sings a wild, sweet song that throbs with pain,
    The added pain of life that transcends art
A song of home, a deep, celestial strain,
    The glorious swan-song of a dying heart.

A lame tramp comes along the railway track,
    A grizzled dog whose day is nearly done;
He passes, pauses, then comes slowly back
    And listens there—an audience of one.

She sings—her golden voice is passion-fraught,
    As when she charmed a thousand eager ears.
He listens trembling, and she knows it not,
    And down his hollow cheeks roll bitter tears.

She ceases and is still, as if to pray;
    There is no sound, the stars are all alight
Only a wretch who stumbles on his way,
    Only a vagrant sobbing in the night.

Small clapboard storefronts lined the streets of Dawson and other towns, and businesses replaced one another on what seemed a daily basis as Yukon entrepreneurs took their lumps or their profits and moved on. Bicycles were common—especially in winter, when it was possible to pedal across frozen rivers and lakes.

The Ballad of Hard-Luck Henry

Now wouldn't you expect to find
    a man an awful crank
That's staked out nigh three hundred claims,
    and every one a blank;
That's followed every fool stampede,
    and seen the rise and fall
Of camps where men got gold in chunks
    and he got none at all;
That's prospected a bit of ground
    and sold it for a song
To see it yield a fortune to
    some fool that came along;
That's sunk a dozen bedrock holes,
    and not a speck in sight,
Yet sees them take a million
    from the claims to left and right?
Now aren't things like that enough
    to drive a man to booze?
But Hard-Luck Smith was hoodoo-proof—
    he knew the way to lose.

'Twas in the fall of nineteen-four—
    leap-year, I've heard them say—
When Hard-Luck came to Hunker Creek
    and took a hillside lay.

And lo! as if to make amends
    for all the futile past,
Late in the year he struck it rich,
    the real pay-streak at last.

The riffles of his sluicing-box
    were choked with speckled earth,
And night and day he worked that lay
    for all that he was worth.
And when in chill December's gloom
    his lucky lease expired,
He found that he had made a stake
    as big as he desired.

One day while meditating on
    the waywardness of fate,
He felt the ache of lonely man
    to find a fitting mate;
A petticoated pard to cheer
    his solitary life,
A woman with soft, soothing ways,
    a confidant, a wife.
And while he cooked his supper
    on his little Yukon stove,
He wished that he had staked a claim
    in Love's rich treasure-trove;
When suddenly he paused and held
    aloft a Yukon egg,
For there in pencilled letters
    was the magic name of Peg.

You know these Yukon eggs of ours—
    some pink, some green, some blue—
A dollar per, assorted tints, assorted flavors, too!

The supercilious cheechako
    might designate them high,
        But one acquires a taste for them
and likes them by-and-by.
        Well, Hard-Luck Henry took this egg
and held it to the light,
        And there was more faint pencilling
that sorely taxed his sight.
        At last he made it out, and then
the legend ran like this—
"Will Klondike miner write to Peg,
        Plumhollow, Squashville, Wis.?"

That night he got to thinking of
        this far-off, unknown fair;
        It seemed so sort of opportune,
        an answer to his prayer.
She flitted sweetly through his dreams,
        she haunted him by day,
She smiled through clouds of nicotine,
        she cheered his weary way.
At last he yielded to the spell;
        his course of love he set—
Wisconsin his objective point,
        his object, Margaret.

With every mile of sea and land
        his longing grew and grew.
He practiced all his pretty words,
        and these, I fear, were few.
At last, one frosty evening,
        with a cold chill down his spine,
He found himself before her house,
        the threshold of the shrine.

His courage flickered to a spark,
        then glowed with sudden flame.
He knocked; he heard a welcome word;
        she came—his goddess came!
Oh, she was fair as any flower,
        and huskily he spoke:
"I'm all the way from Klondike, with
        a mighty heavy poke.
I'm looking for a lassie, one
        whose Christian name is Peg,
Who sought a Klondike miner,
        and who wrote it on an egg."

The lassie gazed at him a space,
        her cheeks grew rosy red.
She gazed at him with tear-bright eyes,
        then tenderly she said:
"Yes, lonely Klondike miner,
        it is true my name is Peg.
It's also true I longed for you
        and wrote it on an egg.
My heart went out to someone in
        that land of night and cold;
But oh, I fear that Yukon egg
        must have been mighty old.
I waited long, I hoped and feared;
        you should have come before;
I've been a wedded woman now
        for eighteen months or more.
I'm sorry, since you've come so far,
        you ain't the one that wins;
But won't you take a step inside?
        I'll let you see the twins!"

Young and old alike caught gold fever in the Yukon.

The Lure of Little Voices

There's a cry from out the loneliness—
    oh, listen, Honey, listen!
Do you hear it, do you fear it?
    You're a-holding of me so;
You're a-sobbing in your sleep, dear,
    and your lashes, how they glisten!—
Do you hear the Little Voices
    all a-begging me to go?

All a-begging me to leave you.
    Day and night they're pleading, praying,
On the North-wind, on the West-wind,
    from the peak and from the plain;
Night and day they never leave me—
    do you know what they are saying?
"He was ours before you got him,
    and we want him once again."

Yes, they're wanting me, they're haunting me,
    the awful lonely places;
They're whining and they're whimpering
    as if each one had a soul;
They're calling from the wilderness,
    the vast and God-like spaces,
The stark and sullen solitudes
    that sentinel the Pole.

They miss my little camp-fires,
    ever brightly, bravely gleaming
In the womb of desolation,
    where was never man before;
As comradeless I sought them,
    lion-hearted, loving, dreaming,
And they hailed me as a comrade,
    and they loved me evermore.

And now they're all a-crying,
    and it's no use me denying;
The spell of them is on me,
    and I'm helpless as a child;
My heart is aching, aching,
    but I hear them, sleeping, waking;
It's the Lure of Little Voices,
    it's the mandate of the Wild.

I'm afraid to tell you, Honey,
    I can take no bitter leaving;
But softly in the sleep-time
    from your love I'll steal away.
Oh, it's cruel, Dearie, cruel,
    and it's God knows how I'm grieving;
But His loneliness is calling,
    and He knows I must obey.

Premonition

'Twas a year ago and the moon was bright
   (Oh, I remember so well, so well);
I walked with my love in a sea of light,
    And the voice of my sweet was a silver bell.
     And sudden the moon grew strangely dull,
      And sudden my love had taken wing;
   I looked on the face of a grinning skull,
     I strained to my heart a ghastly thing.

'Twas but fantasy, for my love lay still
   In my arms, with her tender eyes aglow,
And she wondered why my lips were chill,
   Why I was silent and kissed her so.
    A year has gone and the moon is bright,
     A gibbous moon, like a ghost of woe;
   I sit by a new-made grave tonight,
     And my heart is broken—it's strange, you know.

Although this looks like a California-style photo of a grizzled miner and mine entrance, it's actually post-gold rush Klondike of 1912, long after the rush was past its prime and some 90 percent of the would-be millionaires had left.

The Spell of the Yukon

I wanted the gold, and I sought it;
   I scrabbled and mucked like a slave.
Was it famine or scurvy, I fought it;
   I hurled my youth into a grave.
I wanted the gold, and I got it
   Came out with a fortune last fall,
Yet somehow life's not what I thought it,
   And somehow the gold isn't all.

No! There's the land. (Have you seen it?)
   It's the cussedest land that I know,
From the big, dizzy mountains that screen it
   To the deep, deathlike valleys below.
Some say God was tired when He made it;
   Some say it's a fine land to shun;
Maybe; but there's some as would trade it
   For no land on earth—and I'm one.

You come to get rich (damned good reason);
   You feel like an exile at first.
You hate it like hell for a season,
   And then you are worse than the worst.
It grips you like some kinds of sinning;
   It twists you from foe to a friend;
It seems it's been since the beginning;
   It seems it will be to the end.

I've stood on some mighty-mouthed hollow
   That's plumb-full of hush to the brim.
I've watched the big, husky sun wallow
   In crimson and gold, and grow dim,
Till the moon set the pearly peaks gleaming,
   And the stars tumbled out, neck and crop;
And I've thought that I surely was dreaming,
   With the peace o' the world piled on top.

The summer—no sweeter was ever;
    The sunshiny woods all athrill;
The grayling aleap in the river,
    The bighorn asleep on the hill.
The strong life that never knows harness;
    The wilds where the caribou call;
The freshness, the freedom, the farness
    O God, how I'm stuck on it all!

The winter! the brightness that blinds you,
    The white land locked tight as a drum,
The cold fear that follows and finds you,
    The silence that bludgeons you dumb.
The snows that are older than history,
    The woods where the weird shadows slant;
The stillness, the moonlight, the mystery,
    I've bade 'em good-bye—but I can't.

There's a land where the mountains are nameless,
    And the rivers all run God knows where;
There are lives that are erring and aimless,
    And deaths that just hang by a hair.

There are hardships that nobody reckons;
    There are valleys unpeopled and still;
There's a land—oh, it beckons and beckons,
    And I want to go back—and I will.

They're making my money diminish;
    I'm sick of the taste of champagne.
Thank God! when I'm skinned to a finish
    I'll pike to the Yukon again.
I'll fight—and you bet it's no sham-fight;
    It's hell! but I've been there before;
And it's better than this by a damn sight—
    So me for the Yukon once more.

There's gold, and it's haunting and haunting,
    It's luring me on as of old;
Yet it isn't the gold that I'm wanting
    So much as just finding the gold.
It's the great, big, broad land 'way up yonder,
    It's the forests where silence has lease,
It's the beauty that thrills me with wonder,
    It's the stillness that fills me with peace.

Men of the High North

Men of the High North, the wild sky is blazing;
  Islands of opal float on silver seas;
Swift splendors kindle, barbaric, amazing
  Pale ports of amber, golden argosies.
Ringed all around us the proud peaks are glowing;
  Fierce chiefs in council, their wigwam the sky;
Far, far below us the big Yukon flowing,
  Like threaded quicksilver, gleams to the eye.

Men of the High North, you who have known it,
  You in whose hearts its splendors have abode;
Can you renounce it, can you disown it?
  Can you forget it, its glory and its goad?
Where is the hardship, where is the pain of it?
  Lost in the limbo of things you've forgot;
Only remain the guerdon and gain of it;
  Zest of the foray, and God, how you fought!

You who have made good, you foreign-faring,
  You money magic to far lands has whirled;
Can you forget those days of vast daring,
  There with your soul on the Top o' the World?
Nights when no peril could keep you awake on
  Spruce boughs you spread for your couch in the snow;
Taste your feasts like the beans and the bacon
  Fried at the campfire at forty below?

Can you remember your huskies all going,
  Barking with joy and their brushes in air;
You in your parka, glad-eyed and glowing,
  Monarch, your subjects the wolf and the bear?
Monarch, your kingdom unravisht and gleaming;
  Mountains your throne, and a river your car;
Crash of a bull moose to rouse you from dreaming;
  Forest your couch, and your candle a star?

You who this faint day the High North is luring
  Unto her vastness, taintlessly sweet;
You who are steel-braced, straight-tipped, enduring,
  Dreadless in danger and dire in defeat:
Honor the High North ever and ever,
  Whether she crown you, or whether she slay;
Suffer her fury, cherish and love her
  He who would rule, he must learn to obey.

Men of the High North, fierce mountains love you;
  Proud rivers leap when you ride on their breast.
See, the austere sky, pensive above you,
  Dons all her jewels to smile on your rest.
Children of Freedom, scornful of frontiers,
  We who are weaklings honor your worth.
Lords of the wilderness, Princes of Pioneers,
  Let's have a rouse that will ring round the earth.

A leisurely afternoon hunting or fishing provided miners with a
quiet time for thinking, and perhaps a good meat for that evening.

The Rhyme of the Remittance Man

There's a four-pronged buck a-swinging
    in the shadow of my cabin,
  And it roamed the velvet valley till today;
But I tracked it by the river,
    and I trailed it in the cover,
  And I killed it on the mountain miles away.
Now I've had my lazy supper,
    and the level sun is gleaming
  On the water where the silver salmon play;
And I light my little corn-cob,
    and I linger, softly dreaming,
  In the twilight, of a land that's far away.

Far away, so faint and far,
    is flaming London, fevered Paris,
  That I fancy I have gained another star;
Far away the din and hurry,
    far away the sin and worry,
  Far away—God knows they cannot be too far.
Gilded galley-slaves of Mammon—
    how my purse-proud brothers taunt me!
  I might have been as well-to-do as they
Had I clutched like them my chances,
    learned their wisdom, crushed my fancies,
  Starved my soul and gone to business every day.

Well, the cherry bends with blossom
    and the vivid grass is springing,
  And the star-like lily nestles in the green;
And the frogs their joys are singing,
    and my heart in tune is ringing,
  And it doesn't matter what I might have been.

While above the scented pine-gloom,
    piling heights of golden glory,
  The sun-god paints his canvas in the west,
I can couch me deep in clover,
    I can listen to the story
  Of the lazy, lapping water—it is best.

While the trout leaps in the river,
    and the blue grouse thrills the cover,
  And the frozen snow betrays the panther's track,
And the robin greets the dayspring
    with the rapture of a lover,
  I am happy, and I'll nevermore go back.
For I know I'd just be longing
    for the little old log cabin,
  With the morning-glory clinging to the door,
Till I loathed the city places,
    cursed the care on all the faces,
  Turned my back on lazar London evermore.

So send me far from Lombard Street,
    and write me down a failure;
  Put a little in my purse and leave me free.
Say: "He turned from Fortune's offering
    to follow up a pale lure,
  He is one of us no longer—let him be."
I am one of you no longer;
    by the trails my feet have broken,
  The dizzy peaks I've scaled, the camp-fire's glow;
By the lonely seas I've sailed in—
    yea, the final word is spoken,
  I am signed and sealed to nature. Be it so.

The Cremation of Sam McGee

There are strange things done in the midnight sun
  By the men who moil for gold;
The Arctic trails have their secret tales
  That would make your blood run cold,
The Northern Lights have seen queer sights,
  But the queerest they ever did see
Was that night on the marge of Lake Lebarge
  I cremated Sam McGee.

Now Sam McGee was from Tennessee,
  where the cotton blooms and blows.
Why he left his home in the South to roam
  'round the Pole, God only knows.
He was always cold, but the land of gold
  seemed to hold him like a spell;
Though he'd often say in his homely way
  that he'd "sooner live in Hell."

On a Christmas Day we were mushing our way
  over the Dawson trail.
Talk of your cold! through the parka's fold
  it stabbed like a driven nail.
If our eyes we'd close, then the lashes froze
  till sometimes we couldn't see,
It wasn't much fun, but the only one
  to whimper was Sam McGee.

And that very night, as we lay packed tight
  in our robes beneath the snow,
And the dogs were fed, and the stars o'erhead
  were dancing heel and toe,
He turned to me, and "Cap," says he,
  "I'll cash in this trip, I guess;
And if I do, I'm asking that you
  won't refuse my last request."

Well, he seemed so low that I couldn't say no;
  then he says with a sort of moan,
"It's the cursed cold, and it's got right hold
  till I'm chilled clean through to the bone.
Yet 'taint being dead—it's my awful dread
  of the icy grave that pains;
So I want you to swear that, foul or fair,
  you'll cremate my last remains."

A pal's last need is a thing to heed,
  so I swore I would not fail;
And we started on at the streak of dawn;
  but God! he looked ghastly pale.
He crouched on the sleigh, and he raved all day
  of his home in Tennessee;
And before nightfall a corpse was all
  that was left of Sam McGee.

There wasn't a breath in that land of death,
  and I hurried, horror-driven,
With a corpse half hid that I couldn't get rid,
  because of a promise given;
It was lashed to the sleigh, and it seemed to say:
  "You may tax your brawn and brains,
But you promised true, and it's up to you
  to cremate these last remains."

Now a promise made is a debt unpaid,
  and the trail has its own stern code.
In the days to come, though my lips were dumb
  in my heart how I cursed that load!
In the long, long night, by the lone firelight,
  while the huskies, round in a ring,
Howled out their woes to the homeless snows—
  Oh God, how I loathed the thing!

And every day that quiet clay
    seemed to heavy and heavier grow;
And on I went, though the dogs were spent
    and the grub was getting low.
The trail was bad, and I felt half mad,
    but I swore I would not give in;
And I'd often sing to the hateful thing,
    and it hearkened with a grin.
Till I came to the marge of Lake Lebarge,
    and a derelict there lay;
It was jammed in the ice, but I saw in a trice
    it was called the Alice May,
And I looked at it, and I thought a bit,
    and I looked at my frozen chum;
Then "Here," said I, with a sudden cry,
    "is my cre-ma-tor-eum!"

Some planks I tore from the cabin floor,
    and I lit the boiler fire;
Some coal I found that was lying around,
    and I heaped the fuel higher;
The flames just soared, and the furnace roared—
    such a blaze you seldom see,
And I burrowed a hole in the glowing coal,
    and I stuffed in Sam McGee.

Then I made a hike, for I didn't like
    to hear him sizzle so;
And the heavens scowled, and the huskies howled,
    and the wind began to blow.

It was icy cold, but the hot sweat rolled
    down my cheeks, and I don't know why;
And the greasy smoke in an inky cloak
    went streaking down the sky.

I do not know how long in the snow
    I wrestled with grisly fear;
But the stars came out and they danced about
    ere again I ventured near;
I was sick with dread, but I bravely said,
    "I'll just take a peep inside.
I guess he's cooked, and it's time I looked."
    Then the door I opened wide.

And there sat Sam, looking cool and calm,
    in the heart of the furnace roar;
And he wore a smile you could see a mile,
    and he said, "Please close that door.
It's fine in here, but I greatly fear
    you'll let in the cold and storm—
Since I left Plumtree, down in Tennessee,
    it's the first time I've been warm."

There are strange things done in the midnight sun
    By the men who moil for gold;
The Arctic, trails have their secret tales
    That would make your blood run cold;
The North Lights have seen queer sights,
    But the queerest they ever did see
Was that night on the marge of Lake Lebarge
    I cremated Sam McGee.

Roadhouses provided beds, food, and a brief rest.

The Ballad of Blasphemous Bill

I took a contract to bury the body
    of blasphemous Bill MacKie,
  Whenever, wherever or whatsoever
    the manner of death he die
Whether he die in the light o'day
    or under the peak-faced moon;
  In cabin or dance-hall, camp or dive,
    mucklucks or patent shoon;
On velvet tundra or virgin peak,
    by glacier, drift or draw;
  In muskeg hollow or canyon gloom,
    by avalanche, fang or claw;
By battle, murder or sudden wealth,
    by pestilence, "hooch" or lead
  I swore on the Book I would follow and look
    till I found my tombless dead.

For Bill was a dainty kind of cuss,
    and his mind was mighty sot
  On a dinky patch with flowers and grass
    in a civilized boneyard lot.
And where he died or how he died,
    it didn't matter a damn
  So long as he had a grave with frills
    and a tombstone epigram.
So I promised him, and he paid the price
    in good cheechako coin
  (Which the same I blowed on that very night
    down in the Tenderloin).
Then I painted a three-foot slab of pine:
    "Here lies poor Bill MacKie,"
  And I hung it up on my cabin wall
    and I waited for Bill to die.

Years passed away, and at last one day
    came a squaw with a story strange,
  Of a long-deserted line of traps
    'way back of the Bighorn range;
Of a little hut by the great divide,
    and a white man stiff and still,
  Lying there by his lonesome self,
    and I figured it must be Bill.
So I thought of the contract I'd made with him,
    and I took down from the shelf
  The swell black box with the silver plate
    he'd picked out for hisself;
And I packed it full of grub and "hooch,"
    and I slung it on the sleigh;
  Then I harnessed up my team of dogs
    and was off at dawn of day.

You know what it's like in the Yukon wild
    when it's sixty-nine below;
  When the ice-worms wriggle their purple heads
    through the crust of the pale blue snow;
When the pine trees crack like little guns
    in the silence of the wood,
  And the icicles hang down like tusks
    under the parka hood;
When the stovepipe smoke breaks sudden off,
    and the sky is weirdly lit,
  And the careless feel of a bit of steel
    burns like a red-hot spit;
When the mercury is a frozen ball,
    and the frost-fiend stalks to kill—
  Well, it was just like that that day
    when I set out to look for Bill.

Oh, the awful hush that seemed to crush
    me down on every hand,
  As I blundered blind with a trail to find
    through that blank and bitter land;

Half dazed, half crazed in the winter wild,
    with its grim heart-breaking woes,
  And the ruthless strife for a grip on life
    that only the sourdough knows!
North by the compass, North I pressed;
    river and peak and plain
  Passed like a dream I slept to lose
    and I waked to dream again.

River and plain and mighty peak—
    and who could stand unawed?
  As their summits blazed, he could stand undazed
    at the foot of the throne of God.
North, aye, North, through a land accurst,
    shunned by the scouring brutes,
  And all I heard was my own harsh word
    and the whine of the malamutes,
Till at last I came to a cabin squat,
    built in the side of a hill,
  And I burst in the door, and there on the floor,
    frozen to death, lay Bill.

Ice, white ice, like a winding-sheet,
    sheathing each smoke-grimed wall;
  Ice on the stove-pipe, ice on the bed,
    ice gleaming over all;
Sparkling ice on the dead man's chest,
    glittering ice in his hair,
  Ice on his fingers, ice in his heart,
    ice in his glassy stare;
Hard as a log and trussed like a frog,
    with his arms and legs outspread.
  I gazed at the coffin I'd brought for him,
    and I gazed at the gruesome dead,
And at last I spoke: "Bill liked his joke;
    but still, goldarn his eyes,
  A man had ought to consider his mates
    in the way he goes and dies."

Have you ever stood in an Arctic hut
    in the shadow of the Pole,
With a little coffin six by three
    and a grief you can't control?
Have you ever sat by a frozen corpse
    that looks at you with a grin,
And that seems to say: "You may try all day,
    but you'll never jam me in"?
I'm not a man of the quitting kind,
    but I never felt so blue
As I sat there gazing at that stiff
    and studying what I'd do.
Then I rose and I kicked off the husky dogs
    that were nosing round about,
And I lit a roaring fire in the stove,
    and I started to thaw Bill out.

Well, I thawed and thawed for thirteen days,
    but it didn't seem no good;
His arms and legs stuck out like pegs,
    as if they was made of wood.
Till at last I said: "It ain't no use—
    he's froze too hard to thaw;

He's obstinate, and he won't lie straight,
    so I guess I got to—saw."
So I sawed off poor Bill's arms and legs,
    and I laid him snug and straight
In the little coffin he picked hisself,
    with the dinky silver plate;
And I came nigh near to shedding a tear
    as I nailed him safely down;
Then I stowed him away in my Yukon sleigh,
    and I started back to town.

So I buried him as the contract called
    in a narrow grave and deep,
And there he's waiting the Great Clean-up,
    when the Judgment sluice-heads sweep;
And I smoke my pipe and meditate
    in the light of the Midnight Sun,
And sometimes I wonder if they was,
    the awful things I done.
And as I sit and the parson talks,
    expounding on the Law,
I often think of poor old Bill—
    and how hard he was to saw.

DOMINION DAY BONANZA, Y.T. 1902

KINSEY & KINSEY. PHOTO.

Canadian Dominion Day and the Fourth of July were celebrated with equal fervor by the international population of the Klondike.

The Tramps

Can you recall, dear comrade,
    when we tramped God's land together,
And we sang the old, old Earth-song,
    for our youth was very sweet;
When we drank and fought and lusted,
    as we mocked at tie and tether,
Along the road to Anywhere, the wide world at our feet—

Along the road to Anywhere,
    when each day had its story;
When time was yet our vassal,
    and life's jest was still unstale;
When peace unfathomed filled our hearts as,
    bathed in amber glory,
Along the road to Anywhere we watched the sunsets pale?

Alas! the road to Anywhere
    is pitfalled with disaster;
There's hunger, want, and weariness,
    yet Oh, we loved it so!
As on we tramped exultantly,
    and no man was our master,
And no man guessed what dreams were ours
    as, swinging heel and toe,
We tramped the road to Anywhere,
    the magic road to Anywhere,
The tragic road to Anywhere, such dear, dim years ago.

Grin

If you're up against a bruiser
    and you're getting knocked about—
                  Grin.
If you're feeling pretty groggy,
    and you're licked beyond a doubt—
                  Grin.
Don't let him see you're funking,
    let him know with every clout,
Though your face is battered to a pulp,
    your blooming heart is stout;
Just stand upon your pins until
    the beggar knocks you out—
                And grin.

This life's a bally battle, and
    the same advice holds true
                Of grin.
If you're up against it badly,
    then it's only one on you
                So grin.
If the future's black as thunder,
    don't let people see you're blue;
Just cultivate a cast-iron smile
    of joy the whole day through;

If they call you "Little Sunshine,"
    wishing *they'd* no troubles, too—
                You may—grin.
Rise up in the morning with
    the will that, smooth or rough,
                You'll grin.
Sink to sleep at midnight, and
    although you're feeling tough,
                Yet grin.

There's nothing gained by whining,
    and you're not that kind of stuff;
You're a fighter from away back,
    and you won't take a rebuff;
Your trouble is that you don't know
    when you have had enough
                Don't give in.
If Fate should down you, just get up
    and take another cuff;
You may bank on it that there is no
    philosophy like bluff,
                And grin.

Mining was often done by a husband-and-wife team. But in this case, it was all for show. The woman on the left is definitely dressed for her parlor, not the mine where she is supposedly working with miner-photographer Clarence Kinsey.

The Heart of the Sourdough

There, where the mighty mountains bare
    their fangs unto the moon,
There, where the sullen sun-dogs glare
    in the snow-bright, bitter noon,
And the glacier-glutted streams sweep down
    at the clarion call of June.

There, where the livid tundras keep
    their tryst with the tranquil snows;
There, where the silences are spawned,
    and the light of hell-fire flows
Into the bowl of the midnight sky, violet, amber and rose.

There, where the rapids churn and roar,
    and the ice-floes bellowing run;
Where the tortured, twisted rivers of blood
    rush to the setting sun
I've packed my kit and I'm going, boys,
    ere another day is done.

I knew it would call, or soon or late,
    as it calls the whirring wings;
It's the olden lure, it's the golden lure,
    it's the lure of the timeless things,
And tonight, oh, God of the trails untrod,
    how it whines in my heart-strings!

I'm sick to death of your well-groomed gods,
    your make-believe and your show;
I long for a whiff of bacon and beans,
    a snug shakedown in the snow;
A trail to break, and a life at stake,
    and another bout with the foe.

With the raw-ribbed Wild that abhors all life,
    the Wild that would crush and rend,
I have clinched and closed with the naked North,
    I have learned to defy and defend;
Shoulder to shoulder we have fought it out—
    yet the Wild must win in the end.

I have flouted the Wild. I have followed its lure,
    fearless, familiar, alone;
By all that the battle means and makes
    I claim that land for mine own;
Yet the Wild must win, and a day will come
    when I shall be overthrown.

Then when, as wolf-dogs fight, we've fought,
    the lean wolf-land and I;
Fought and bled till the snows are red
    under the reeling sky;
Even as lean wolf-dogs go down
    will I go down and die.

The Little Old Log Cabin

When a man gits on his uppers in a hard-pan sort of town,
  An' he ain't got nothin' comin'
    an' he can't afford ter eat,
An' he's in a fix for lodgin'
    an' he wanders up an' down,
  An' you'd fancy he'd been boozin',
    he's so locoed 'bout the feet;
When he's feelin' sneakin' sorry
    an' his belt is hangin' slack,
  An' his face is peaked an' gray-like
    an' his heart gits down an' whines,
Then he's apt ter git a-thinkin'
    an' a-wishin' he was back
In the little ol' log cabin in the shadder of the pines.

When he's on the blazin' desert an' his canteen's sprung a leak,
  An' he's all alone an' crazy
    an' he's crawlin' like a snail,
An' his tongue's so black an' swollen
    that it hurts him fer to speak,
  An' he gouges down fer water
    an' the raven's on his trail;
When he's done with care and cursin'
    an' he feels more like to cry,

An' he sees ol' Death a-grinnin'
    an' he thinks upon his crimes,
Then he's like ter hev' a vision,
    as he settles down ter die,
  Of the little ol' log cabin an' the roses an' the vines.

Oh, the little ol' log cabin, it's a solemn shinin' mark,
  When a feller gits ter sinnin'
    an' a-goin' ter the wall,
An' folks don't understand him
    an' he's gropin' in the dark,
  An' he's sick of bein' cursed at
    an' he's longin' fer his call!
When the sun of life's a-sinkin'
    you can see it 'way above,
  On the hill from out the shadder
    in a glory 'ginst the sky,
An' your mother's voice is callin',
    an' her arms are stretched in love,
An' somehow you're glad you're goin,
    an' you ain't a-scared to die;
When you'll be like a kid again
    an' nestle to her breast,
  An' never leave its shelter, an' forget, an' love, an' rest.

The Parson's Son

This is the song of the Parson's son,
*   as he squats in his shack alone,*
On the wild, weird nights, when the Northern Lights
*   shoot up from the frozen zone,*
And it's sixty below, and couched in the snow
*   the hungry huskies moan.*

"I'm one of the Arctic brotherhood,
    I'm an old-time pioneer.
  I came with the first—O God, how I've cursed
    this Yukon!—but still I'm here.
I've sweated athirst in its summer heat,
    I've frozen and starved in its cold;
  I've followed my dreams by its thousand streams,
    I've toiled and moiled for its gold.

"Look at my eyes—been snow-blind twice—
    look where my foot's half gone;
  And that gruesome scar on my left cheek, where
    the frost-fiend bit to the bone.
Each one a brand of this devil's land,
    where I've played and I've lost the game,
  A broken wreck with a craze for 'hooch,'
    and never a cent to my name.

"This mining is only a gamble;
    the worst is as good as the best.
  I was in with the bunch and I might have come out
    right on top with the rest;
With Cormack, Ladue and Macdonald—
    O God! but it's Hell to think
  Of the thousands and thousands I've squandered
    on cards and women and drink.

"In the early days we were just a few,
      and we hunted and fished around,
Ne'er dreamt by our lonely campfires
      of the wealth that lay under the ground.
We traded in skins and whiskey,
      and I've often slept under the shade
Of that lone birch tree on Bonanza,
      where the first big find was made.

"We were just like a great big family,
      and every man had his squaw,
And we lived such a wild, free, fearless life
      beyond the pale of the law;
Till sudden there came a whisper,
      and it maddened us every man,
And I got in on Bonanza
      before the big rush began.

"Oh, those Dawson days, and the sin and the blaze,
      and the town all open wide!
(If God made me in His likeness,
      sure He let the devil inside.)
But we all were mad, both the good and the bad,
      and as for the women, well—
No spot on the map in so short a space
      has hustled more souls to Hell.

"Money was just like dirt there,
      easy to get and to spend.
I was all caked in on a dance-hall jade,
      but she shook me in the end.
It put me queer, and for near a year
      I never drew sober breath,
Till I found myself in the bughouse ward
      with a claim staked out on death.

"Twenty years in the Yukon,
      struggling along its creeks;
Roaming its giant valleys,
      scaling its god-like peaks;
Bathed in its fiery sunsets,
      fighting its fiendish cold
Twenty years in the Yukon . . .
      twenty years—and I'm old.

"Old and weak, but no matter,
      there's 'hooch' in the bottle still.
I'll hitch up the dogs tomorrow,
      and mush down the trail to Bill.
It's so long dark, and I'm lonesome—
      I'll just lay down on the bed;
Tomorrow I'll go . . . tomorrow . . .
      I guess I'll play on the red.

"—Come, Kit, your pony is saddled.
      I'm waiting, dear, in the court . . .
—Minnie, you devil, I'll kill you
      if you skip with that flossy sport . . .
—How much does it go to the pan, Bill? . . .
      play up, School, and play the game . . .
—Our Father, which art in heaven,
      hallowed be Thy name . . ."

This was the song of the parson's son,
      as he lay in his bunk alone,
Ere the fire went out and the cold crept in,
      and his blue lips ceased to moan,
And the hunger-maddened malamutes
      had torn him flesh from bone.

Time to relax and reflect on another winter's cleanup.

The Law of the Yukon

This is the law of the Yukon,
      and ever she makes it plain:
  "Send not your foolish and feeble;
      send me your strong and your sane—
Strong for the red rage of battle;
      sane, for I harry them sore;
  Send me men girt for the combat,
      men who are grit to the core;
Swift as the panther in triumph,
      fierce as the bear in defeat,
  Sired of a bulldog parent,
      steeled in the furnace heat.

"Send me the best of your breeding,
      lend me your chosen ones;
  Them will I take to my bosom,
      them will I call my sons;
Them will I gild with my treasure,
      them will I glut with my meat;
  But the others—the misfits, the failures—
      I trample them under my feet.
Dissolute, damned and despairful,
      crippled and palsied and stain,
  Ye would send me the spawn of your gutters—
      Go take back your spawn again!

"Wild and wide are my borders,
      stern as death is my sway;
  From my ruthless throne I have ruled alone
      for a million years and a day;
Hugging my mighty treasure,
      waiting for man to come,
  Till he swept like a turbid torrent,
      and after him swept the scum.

The pallid pimp of the dead-line,
 the enervate of the pen,
 One by one I weeded them out,
  for all that I sought was—Men.

"One by one I dismayed them,
 frighting them sore with my glooms;
 One by one I betrayed them
  unto my manifold dooms.
Drowned them like rats in my rivers,
 starved them like cuts on my plains,
 Rotted the flesh that was left them,
  poisoned the blood in their veins;
Burst with my winter upon them,
 searing forever their sight,
 Lashed them with fungus-white faces,
  whimpering wild in the night;

Staggering blind through the storm-whirl,
 stumbling mad through the snow,
 Frozen stiff in the ice-pack,
  brittle and bent like a bow;
Featureless, formless, forsaken,
 scented by wolves in their flight,
 Left for the wind to make music,
  through ribs that are glittering white;
Gnawing the black crust of failure,
 searching the pit of despair,
 Crooking the toe in the trigger,
  trying to patter a prayer;

"Going outside with an escort,
 raving with lips all afoam,
 Writing a check for a million,
  driveling feebly of home;
Lost like a louse in the burning . . .
  or else in the tented town

Seeking a drunkard's solace,
 sinking and sinking down;
 Steeped in the slime at the bottom,
  dead to a decent world,
 Lost 'mid the human flotsam,
  far on the frontier hurled;

"In the camp at the bend of the river,
 with its dozen saloons aglare,
 Its gambling dens ariot,
  its gramophones all ablare;
Crimped with the crimes of a city,
 sin-ridden and bridled with lies,
 In the hush of my mountained vastness,
  in the flush of my midnight skies.
Plague-spots, yet tools of my purpose,
 so natheless I suffer them thrive,
 Crushing my Weak in their clutches,
  that only my Strong may survive.

"But the others, the men of my mettle,
 the men who would 'stablish my fame
 Unto its ultimate issue,
  winning me honor, not shame;
Searching my uttermost valleys,
 fighting each step as they go.
 Shooting the wrath of my rapids,
  scaling my ramparts of snow;

Ripping the guts of my mountains,
 looting the beds of my creeks,
 Them will I take to my bosom,
  and speak as a mother speaks.
I am the land that listens,
 I am the land that broods;
 Steeped in eternal beauty,
  crystalline waters and woods.

Long have I waited lonely,
    shunned as a thing accurst,
Monstrous, moody, pathetic,
    the last of the lands and the first;
Visioning campfires at twilight,
    sad with a longing forlorn,
Feeling my womb o'er-pregnant
    with the seed of cities unborn.

"Wild and wide are my borders,
    stern as death is my sway,
And I wait for the men who will win me—
    and will not be won in a day;
And I will not be won by weaklings,
    subtle, suave and mild,
But by men with the hearts of Vikings,
    and the simple faith of a child;
Desperate, strong and resistless,
    unthrottled by fear or defeat,
Them will I gild with my treasure,
    them will I glut with my meat.

"Loftly I stand from each sister land,
    patient and wearily wise,
With the weight of a world of sadness
    in my quiet, passionless eyes;

Dreaming alone of a people,
    dreaming alone of a day,
When men shall not rape my riches,
    and curse me and go away;

Making a bawd of my bounty,
    fouling the hand that gave
Till I rise in my wrath and I sweep on their path
    and I stamp them into a grave;
"Dreaming of men who will bless me,
    of women esteeming me good,
Of children born in my borders
    of radiant motherhood,
Of cities leaping to stature,
    of fame like a flag unfurled,
As I pour the tide of my riches
    in the eager lap of the world."

This is the Law of the Yukon,
    that only the Strong shall thrive;
That surely the Weak shall perish,
    and only the Fit survive.
Dissolute, damned and despairful,
    crippled and palsied and slain,
This is the Will of the Yukon—
    Lo, how she makes it plain!

Dogs were truly a miner's best friend—they provided companionship in the lonely North, and were a vital link between mine and town when the only other option was an arduous hike.

Lost

"Black is the sky, but the land is white—
Oh, the wind, the snow and the storm!
Father, where is our boy tonight?
Pray to God he is safe and warm."

"Mother, mother, why should you fear?
Safe is he, and the Arctic moon
Over his cabin shines so clear—
Rest and sleep, 'twill be morning soon."

"It's getting dark awful sudden.
        Say, this is mighty queer!
    Where in the world have I got to?
        It's still and black as a tomb.
I reckoned the camp was yonder,
        I figured the trail was here—
    Nothing! Just draw and valley
        packed with quiet and gloom;
Snow that comes down like feathers,
        thick and gobby and gray;
    Night that looks spiteful ugly—
        seems that I've lost my way.

"The cold's got an edge like a jackknife—
        it must be forty below;
    Leastways that's what it seems like—
        it cuts so fierce to the bone.
The wind's getting real ferocious;
        it's heaving and whirling the snow;
    It shrieks with a howl of fury,
        it dies away to a moan;
Its arms sweep round like a banshee's,
        swift and icily white,
    And buffet and blind and beat me.
        Lord! it's a hell of a night.

"I'm all tangled up in a blizzard.
        There's only one thing to do—
    Keep on moving and moving;
        it's death, it's death if I rest.
Oh, God! if I see the morning,
        if only I struggle through,
    I'll say the prayers I've forgotten
        since I lay on my mother's breast.
I seem going round in a circle;
        maybe the camp is near.
    Say! did somebody holler?
        Was it a light I saw?
Or was it only a notion?
        I'll shout, and maybe they'll hear
    No! the wind only drowns me—
        shout till my throat is raw.

"The boys are all round the camp-fire
        wondering when I'll be back.
    They'll soon be starting to seek me;
        they'll scarcely wait for the light.
What will they find, I wonder,
        when they come to the end of my track—
    A hand stuck out of a snowdrift,
        frozen and stiff and white.
That's what they'll strike, I reckon;
        that's how they'll find their pard,
    A pie-faced corpse in a snowbank
        curse you, don't be a fool!
Play the game to the finish;
        bet on your very last card;
    Nerve yourself for the struggle.
        Oh, you coward, keep cool!

"I'm going to lick this blizzard;
 I'm going to live the night.
It can't down me with its bluster—
 I'm not the kind to be beat.
On hands and knees will I buck it;
 with every breath will I fight;
It's life, it's life that I fight for—
 never it seemed so sweet.
I know that my face is frozen;
 my hands are numblike and dead;
But oh, my feet keep a-moving,
 heavy and hard and slow;
They're trying to kill me, kill me,
 the night that's black overhead,
The wind that cuts like a razor,
 the whipcord lash of the snow.

"Keep a-moving, a-moving,
 don't, don't stumble, you fool!
Curse this snow that's a-piling
 a-purpose to block my way.
It's heavy as gold in the rocker,
 it's white and fleecy as wool;
It's soft as a bed of feathers,
 it's warm as a stack of hay.
Curse on my feet that slip so,
 my poor tired, stumbling feet
I guess they're a job for the surgeon,
 they feel so queerlike to lift
I'll rest them just for a moment—
 oh, but to rest is sweet!
The awful wind cannot get me,
 deep, deep down in the drift."

"Father, a bitter cry I heard,
 Out of the night so dark and wild.
Why is my heart so strangely stirred?
 'Twas like the voice of our erring child."

"Mother, mother, you only heard
 A waterfowl in the locked lagoon
Out of the night a wounded bird
 Rest and sleep, 'twill be morning soon."

'Who is it talks of sleeping?
 I'll swear that somebody shook
Me hard by the arm for a moment,
 but how on earth could it be?
See how my feet are moving—
 awfully funny they look—
Moving as if they belonged
 to a someone that wasn't me.
The wind down the night's long alley
bowls me down like a pin;
 I stagger and fall and stagger,
 crawl arm-deep in the snow.
Beaten back to my corner,
 how can I hope to win?
And there is the blizzard waiting
 to give me the knockout blow.
"Oh, I'm so warm and sleepy!
 No more hunger and pain.
Just to rest for a moment;
 was ever rest such a joy?
Ha! what was that? I'll swear it,
 somebody shook me again;
Somebody seemed to whisper:
 "Fight to the last, my boy."
Fight! That's right, I must struggle.
 I know that to rest means death;
Death, but then what does death mean?
 ease from a world of strife.
Life has been none too pleasant;
 yet with my failing breath
Still and still must I struggle,
 fight for the gift of life . . .

"Seems that I must be dreaming!
    Here is the old home trail;
Yonder a light is gleaming;
    oh, I know it so well!
The air is scented with clover;
    the cattle wait by the rail;
Father is through with the milking;
    there goes the supper-bell . . .
Mother, your boy is crying,
    out in the night and cold;
Let me in and forgive me,
    I'll never be bad any more;
I'm, oh, so sick and so sorry;
    please, dear mother, don't scold—

It's just your boy, and he wants you . . .
    Mother, open the door . . ."

"Father, father, I saw a face
    Pressed just now to the window-pane!
Oh, it gazed for a moment's space,
    Wild and wan, and was gone again!"

"Mother, mother, you saw the snow
    Drifted down from the maple tree
Oh, the wind that is sobbing so!
    Weary and worn and old are we—
Only the snow and a wounded loon.
    Rest and sleep, 'twill be morning soon.

The grub tent was
austere, but it was a
welcome source of
food and friendship
after long hours
of mining.

L'Envoi
[1909]

We talked of yesteryears, of trails and treasure,
    Of men who played the game and lost or won;
Of mad stampedes, of toil beyond all measure,
    Of camp-fire comfort when the day was done.
      We talked of sullen nights by moon-dogs haunted,
        Of bird and beast and tree, of rod and gun;
    Of boat and tent, of hunting-trip enchanted
      Beneath the wonder of the midnight sun;
Of bloody-footed dogs that gnawed the traces,
    Of prisoned seas, wind-lashed and winter-locked;
The ice-gray dawn was pale upon our faces,
    Yet still we filled the cup and still we talked.

The city street was dimmed. We saw the glitter
    Of moon-picked brilliants on the virgin snow,
And down the drifted canyon heard the bitter,
    Relentless slogan of the winds of woe.
      The city was forgot, and, parka-skirted,
        We trod that leagueless land that once we knew.
    We saw stream past, down valleys glacier-girted,
      The wolf-worn legions of the caribou.
We smoked our pipes, o'er scenes of triumph dwelling,
    Of deeds of daring, dire defeats, we talked;
And other tales that lost not in the telling,
    Ere to our beds uncertainly we walked.

And so, dear friends, in gentler valleys roaming,
    Perhaps, when on my printed page you look,
Your fancies by the firelight may go homing
    To that lone land that haply you forsook.
      And if perchance you hear the silence calling,
        The frozen music of star-yearning heights,
    Or, dreaming, see the seines of silver trawling
      Across the sky's abyss on vasty nights,
You may recall that sweep of savage splendor,
    That land that measures each man at his worth,
And feel in memory, half fierce, half tender,
    The brotherhood of men that know the North.

GLOSSARY

Arcadie	Pastoral region of ancient Greece that came to be considered a rural, bucolic paradise.
argently	In a silvery-white way.
attainted	Convicted; sullied, disgraced.
bally	Synonym for "bloody."
bull-pines	Long-needled pine; e.g., ponderosa, digger, loblolly or limber pine.
calcined	Reduced to whitish powder by intense heat.
canorous	Suggestive of loud, swelling song.
canvas-back	Wild duck with salt-and-pepper back plumage.
chancel rat	Larger cousin of the churchmouse.
cheechako	[Chinook:] tenderfoot, greenhorn.
chummed up	Formed a close friendship.
college eight	Crew team representing the school in a race.
coronal	Of the Northern Lights' apparent convergence around the magnetic pole.
Dead-line	Line that a prisoner may not cross, under penalty of being shot by a guard.
defile	Long, narrow pass.
dight	Tidied or spruced up; arranged, put in order.
disprized	Despised.
Drouthy	Dry; craving a drink.
Eldorado	Mythical land where gold is fabulously plentiful.
empery	Dominion; domain; "sphere of influence."
enervate	Weakened, enfeebled, neurasthenic individual.
envoi	Author's explanatory note that concludes a book.
fagged	Worked as an unpaid servant for an older boy in an English public [boarding] school.
fain	Gladly willing.
faro men	Keepers of the "bank" in the card game of faro.
ferine	Fierce; undomesticated.
fleered	Sneered; mocked with a sardonic grimace.
flensing	Able to strip off long ribbons of skin and fat.
flume-head	Start of a wooden trough used to divert water, in mining.
foreloopers	Boys who walk beside the first yoke of a team of oxen to guide them.
frowst	To lounge indoors.
funking	Flinching; holding back out of fear.
gelid	Icy, frigid.
gibbous	Humped, said of the three-quarter moon.
grayling	Salmonlike fish related to the trout.
green stuff	Absinthe, a wormwood-flavored liqueur.

grubstake	Money or provisions advanced to a miner in return for a share in his future claims.
guerdon	Reward; recompense.
helots	Pariahs; serfs; untouchables.
hog-back	Ridge with a sharp summit and steep sides.
hollow needle	Hypodermic used to inject drugs.
"hooch"	Rotgut whiskey; moonshine.
hoodoo	Bad luck; jinx.
husbandmen	Farmhands.
ice-worms	Twigs or branches protruding through the snow and enveloped in ice so as to resemble slimy, segmented creatures.
insensate	Unfeeling; foolish; brutal.
jade	Brassy, shrewish woman.
jag-time	Period of intoxication.
jammy	Delightfully simple or easy.
karroo	High-altitude South African tableland.
klooch	[Chinook:] Indian woman.
knuckle down	In a game of marbles, getting ready to shoot.
lazar	Scabrous, leprous.
lief	Gladly willing.
mackinaw	Heavy woolen blanket, in stripes or solid colors.
marge	Edge; shoreline.
mere	Lake; pond.
mill-race	Flowing water that drives a mill wheel.
moil	Dig under wet, dirty conditions; grub.
Moose-hides	Garments worn by Indians; by extension, derogatory term for the Indians themselves.
muckluck	Boot of reindeer skin, with a soft sole.
mummer	One who goes merrymaking in disguise.
mush	To travel by dogsled.
muskeg	Sphagnum-moss bog.
natheless	Nevertheless.
neck and crop	Swiftly and efficiently; wasting no time.
nigger-head	Hummock or tussock of vegetation: grass, moss, etc.
patent	Patent leather.
pay-streak	Vein of rich ore.
piked	Made one's way.
pinions	Wings; also: gear wheels.

potlatched	Gave lavishly, with the expectation of a gift in return.
ptarmigan	Bird of the grouse family with feathered feet and white winter plumage.
raven, ravin	To seize and devour greedily.
reindeer moss	Upright, branched lichen of a pale grey color.
relays	Small bundles to be cached along one's route and picked up on the return.
riffles	On the bottom of a sluice, grooves to trap and hold nuggets.
sacerdotal	Priestly.
scrofulous	Diseased; contaminated; ulcerous.
seine	Wide, oblong net for herding and trapping fish.
shake	Shake hands; i.e., part company.
shoon	[Scottish:] shoes.
Silver Flail	The Northern Lights.
Siwash	Disparaging term for Indians.
sluice-box	One of the 12-foot units of a gold-mining sluice.
sniped	Hunted and trapped long-billed game birds.
sourdough	Veteran; old-timer; opposite of cheechako.
spread misère	Card game in which the bidder (who is trying to lose every trick) plays with all his cards face up.
stent	Extent.
swell	Member of the upper crust; man about town.
tailings	Crushed rock from which desirable minerals have been extracted.
tallow	The white rendered fat of a cow or sheep suet.
tinhorns	Bragging, pretentious show-offs.
topers	Drunkards.
travail	Painful drudgery; stressful endurance.
tundra sponge	Moss and lichen.
tups and wethers	Rams and male sheep.
upshoaled	Made shallow by a mudbank or sandbar.
vox humana	Reed-pipe organ whose sound imitates the human voice.
wattle-blooms	Acacia flowers.
weal	Well-being; good fortune.
weasened up	Wizened up; puckered.
weft	In a loom thread carried by the shuttle.
weltering	Writhing, tumbling, struggling.
windlass	Drum used to wind rope and thereby raise buckets of water, heavy objects, etc.